HEALING & WELLNESS
Beyond Recovery
Self-Healing to Relieve Anxiety, Addiction, Depression, Grief, Post-Traumatic Stress, and Pain

By Kathleen Riley

Come to the edge.
No, we will fall.

Come to the edge.
No, we will fall.

They came to the edge.
He pushed them, and they flew.

— *Guillaume Apollinaire*

HEALING & WELLNESS
Beyond Recovery

Self-Healing to Relieve Anxiety, Addiction, Depression, Grief, Post-Traumatic Stress, and Pain

By Kathleen Riley

Copyright © 2016, K Riley Agency LLC.

First Edition   ISBN: 978-0-9761936-3-0

All rights reserved. No part of this book may be reproduced, stored in a retrieval system, or transmitted in any form by recording or otherwise without the written permission of K Riley Agency LLC.

Additional copies of this book may be obtained by contacting:

Kathleen Riley

Phone: 248.321.9200 or Email: kriley@thedovehouse.org

Disclaimer: These methods are not intended for use in place of the care of a doctor, medical professional or healthcare provider. Please contact your doctor for any medical concerns or questions you may have pertaining to your health.

Dedicated to My Family and Friends

Thank you for the nurturance and support you gave me
throughout my journey of Healing & Wellness Beyond Recovery

Dr. Billie Beverly

Babette Cain

Susan Kerwin

Dr. Howard Kerwin

Gigi Langer

Marilyn Mitchell

Deb Tierney

Mary Seibert

Dr. David Viviano

Maureen Voughan

Adult Children of Alcoholics/
Dysfunctional Family Group

Table of Contents

One | Assessments | Page 7

Two | Archetypes & Energy Centers | 14

Three | | Creating New Realities | 23

Four | Your Vital Energy | Page 37

Five | Core Healing | Page 46

Six | Energy Strategies | Page 61

Seven | Amends & Forgiveness | Page 77

Eight | Affirmations, Gifts & Gratitude | Page 81

Appendix | Educational Series | Page 87

Twelve Principles of Holistic Medical Practice

1. Unconditional love is life's most powerful healer.
2. Optimal health is much more than the absence of sickness.
3. Illness is viewed as a manifestation of the whole person, not as an isolated event.
4. Holistic physicians embrace a variety of safe, effective options in diagnosis and treatment, including:
    - education for lifestyle changes and self-care
    - complementary approaches; and
    - conventional drugs and surgery.
5. Searching for the underlying cause of disease is preferable to treating symptoms alone.
6. Holistic physicians expend as much effort on establishing what kind of patient has a disease as they do establishing what kind of disease a patient has.
7. Prevention is preferable to treatment and is usually more cost-effective. The most cost-effective approach evokes the patient's own healing capabilities.
8. A major determinant of healing outcomes is the quality of the relationship established between physician and patient, in which patient autonomy is encouraged.
9. The ideal physician-patient relationship considers the needs, desires, awareness and insight of the patient, as well as those of the physician.
10. Physicians significantly influence patients by their examples.
11. Illness, pain and the dying process can be learning opportunities for patients and physicians.
12. Holistic physicians encourage patients to evoke the healing power of love, hope, humor and enthusiasm, and to release the toxic consequences of hostility, shame, greed, depression, and prolonged fear, anger and grief.

Source: The American Board of Holistic Medicine

One
Assessments

ABHM Holistic Health and Wellness Questionnaire

Answer the questions in each section below and total your score. Each response will be a number from 0 to 5.

Note: Please refer to the *frequency* described within parentheses (e.g., 2–3x/week) *only* when answering questions about a *specific activity*, e.g., "Do you maintain a healthy diet?" or "Do you awaken in the morning feeling well-rested?" However, when the question refers to an attitude or an emotion, as in most of the Mind and Spirit questions (e.g., "Do you have a sense of humor?"), the response is more subjective, and you do not need to consider specific frequency in answering the question.

0 = Never or almost never (once a year or less)
1 = Seldom (2–12 times/year)
2 = Occasionally (2–4 times/month)
3 = Often (2–3 times/week)
4 = Regularly (4–6 times/week)
5 = Daily (every day)

BODY: Physical and Environmental Health
____ 1. Do you maintain a healthy diet (low fat, low sugar, fresh fruits, grains and vegetables)?
____ 2. Is your daily water intake adequate (at least 1/2 oz./lb. of body weight; 160 lbs. = 80 oz.)?
____ 3. Are you within 20 percent of your ideal body weight?
____ 4. Do you feel physically attractive?
____ 5. Do you fall asleep easily and sleep soundly?
____ 6. Do you awaken in the morning feeling well-rested?
____ 7. Do you have more than enough energy to meet your daily responsibilities?
____ 8. Are your five senses (smell, taste, sight, hearing, touch) acute?
____ 9. Do you take time to experience sensual pleasure?
____ 10. Do you schedule regular massage or deep-tissue bodywork?
____ 11. Does your sexual relationship feel gratifying?
____ 12. Do you engage in regular physical workouts lasting at least 20 minutes each?
____ 13. Do you have good endurance and aerobic capacity?
____ 14. Do you breathe abdominally for at least a few minutes?
____ 15. Do you maintain physically challenging goals?
____ 16. Are you physically strong?
____ 17. Do you do some stretching exercises?
____ 18. Are you free of chronic aches, pains, ailments and diseases?
____ 19. Do you have regular effortless bowel movements?
____ 20. Do you understand the causes of your chronic physical problems?

____ 21. Are you free of any drug or alcohol dependency (including nicotine and caffeine)?
____ 22. Do you live in a healthy environment with respect to clean air, water and indoor pollution?
____ 23. Do you feel energized and empowered by nature?
____ 24. Do you feel a strong connection to and appreciation for your body, home and environment?
____ 25. Do you have an awareness of life-energy (or "qi")?

TOTAL BODY SCORE _____

0 = Never or almost never (once a year or less)
1 = Seldom (2–12 times/year)
2 = Occasionally (2–4 times/month)
3 = Often (2–3 times/week)
4 = Regularly (4–6 times/week)
5 = Daily (every day)

MIND: Mental and Emotional Health
____ 1. Do you have specific goals in your personal and professional life?
____ 2. Do you have the ability to concentrate for extended periods?
____ 3. Do you use visualization or mental imagery to help you attain your goals or enhance performance?
____ 4. Do you believe it is possible to change?
____ 5. Can you meet your financial needs and desires?
____ 6. Is your outlook optimistic?
____ 7. Do you give yourself more supportive messages than critical messages?
____ 8. Does your job utilize all of your greatest talents?
____ 9. Is your job enjoyable and fulfilling?
____ 10. Are you willing to take risks or make mistakes in order to succeed?
____ 11. Are you able to adjust beliefs and attitudes when learning from painful experiences?
____ 12. Do you have a sense of humor?
____ 13. Do you maintain peace of mind and tranquility?
____ 14. Are you free from a strong need for control or the need to be right?
____ 15. Are you able to fully experience (feel) painful feelings such as fear, anger, sadness and hopelessness?
____ 16. Are you aware of, and able to safely express, fear?

____ 17. Are you aware of, and able to safely express, anger?
____ 18. Are you aware of, and able safely to express, sadness, and/or to cry?
____ 19. Are you accepting of all your feelings?
____ 20. Do you engage in meditation, contemplation or psychotherapy to better understand your feelings?
____ 21. Is your sleep free from disturbing dreams?
____ 22. Do you explore the symbolism and emotional content of your dreams?
____ 23. Do you take time to decompress and relax, or make time for activities that constitute the freedom or absorption of play?
____ 24. Do you experience feelings of exhilaration?
____ 25. Do you enjoy high self-esteem?

TOTAL MIND/EMOTIONS SCORE _____

0 = Never or almost never (once a year or less)
1 = Seldom (2–12 times/year)
2 = Occasionally (2–4 times/month)
3 = Often (2–3 times/week)
4 = Regularly (4–6 times/week)
5 = Daily (every day)

SPIRIT: Spiritual and Social Health

____ 1. Do you actively commit time to your spiritual life?
____ 2. Do you take time for prayer, meditation or reflection?
____ 3. Do you listen to your intuition?
____ 4. Are creative activities a part of your work and/or leisure time?
____ 5. Do you take risks or exceed previous limits?
____ 6. Do you have faith in a God, spirit guides or angels?
____ 7. Are you free from anger toward God?
____ 8. Are you grateful for the blessings in your life?
____ 9. Do you take walks, do gardening or have contact with nature?
____ 10. Are you able to let go of your attachment to specific outcomes and embrace uncertainty?
____ 11. Do you observe a day of rest completely away from work, dedicated to nurturing yourself and/or your family?

____ 12. Can you let go of self-interest in deciding the best course of action for a given situation?
____ 13. Do you feel a sense of purpose?
____ 14. Do you make time to connect with young children, either your own or someone else's?
____ 15. Are playfulness and humor important to you in your daily life?
____ 16. Do you have the ability to forgive yourself and others?
____ 17. Have you demonstrated the willingness to commit to a marriage or compatible long-term relationship?
____ 18. Do you experience intimacy, besides sex, in your committed relationships?
____ 19. Do you confide in or speak openly with one or more close friends?
____ 20. Do you or did you feel close to your parents?
____ 21. If you have experienced the loss of a loved one, have you fully grieved that loss?
____ 22. Has your experience of pain enabled you to grow spiritually?
____ 23. Do you go out of your way for, or give time to help, others?
____ 24. Do you feel a sense of belonging to a group or community?
____ 25. Do you experience unconditional love?

TOTAL SPIRIT SCORE _____

Add up all your scores to find your Body, Mind and Spirit Score _____

HEALTH SCALE
325–375 Optimal Health
275–324 Excellent Health
225–274 Good Health
175–224 Fair Health
125–174 Below Average Health
75–124 Poor Health
0–74 Extremely Poor Health (Surviving)

Energy Analysis

Name:

Date:

7

6

5

4

3

2

1

Energy Analysis

Name:

Date:

7

6

5

4

3

2

1

Two Archetypes & Energy Centers

1. Select twelve archetypes that most closely align with who you are. Everyone has the first four archetypes: victim, prostitute, saboteur and child. Determine which child best describes you and then select eight more types.

   1. Victim
   2. Prostitute
   3. Saboteur
   4. Child (_____)
   5. _____
   6. _____
   7. _____
   8. _____
   9. _____
   10. _____
   11. _____
   12. _____

Healing & Wellness Beyond Recovery

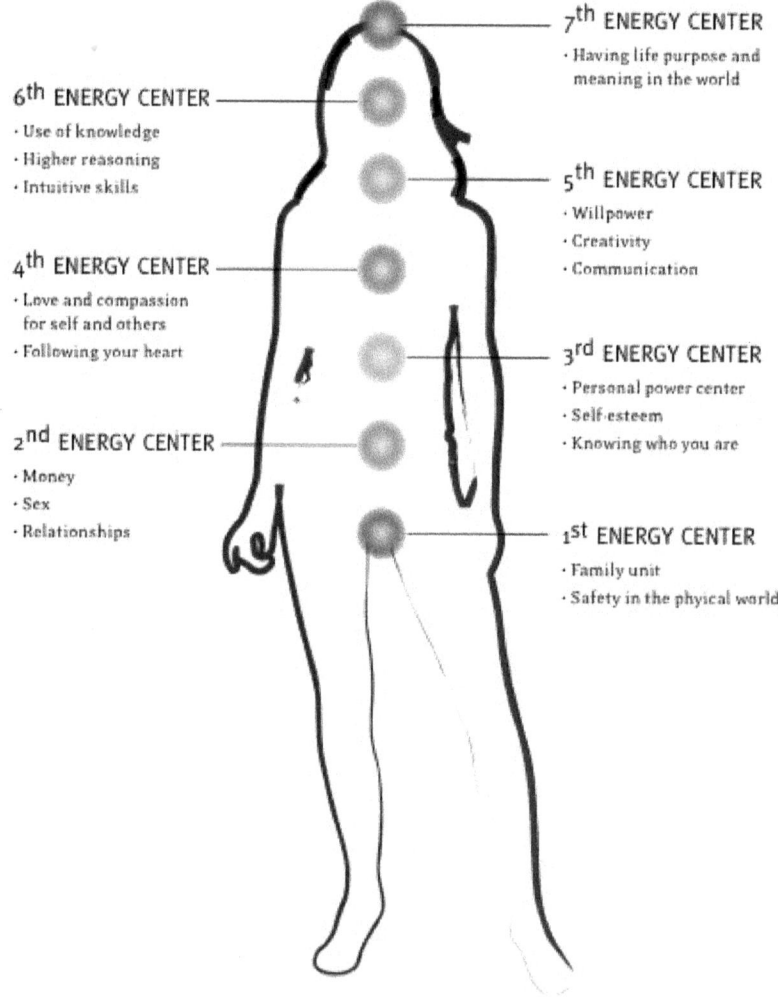

2. Intuitively match each archetype with a number from 1–12. Next, write down the archetype with the corresponding number you have selected. These numbers represent the twelve houses corresponding to the twelve signs of the zodiac and energy centers in your body.

Archetypes	Zodiac Houses & Corresponding Energy Centers
1.	1. Ego & Personality (First through third centers)
2.	2. Life Values (Second center)
3.	3. Self-Expression & Siblings (Third through fifth centers)
4.	4. Home (First through fourth centers)
5.	5. Creativity and Good Fortune (Sixth center)
6.	6. Occupation and Health (Second center)
7.	7. Marriage and Relationships (Second through fourth centers)
8.	8. Other People's Resources (Second through sixth centers)
9.	9. Spirituality (Seventh Center)
10.	10. Highest Potential (Fifth through seventh centers)
11.	11. Relationship to the World (Fourth through sixth centers)
12.	12. The Unconscious (Sixth through seventh centers)

3. Building Your Living Matrix System: Start with the first meta-archetype corresponding to energy centers through 4 (Home) and label your archetype on the Living Matrix System. Next, label your second meta-archetype corresponding to energy centers 2 through 6 (Other People's Resources) on the Living Matrix System. From there, label your diamond ladder archetypes and core energy center archetypes on the Living Matrix System.

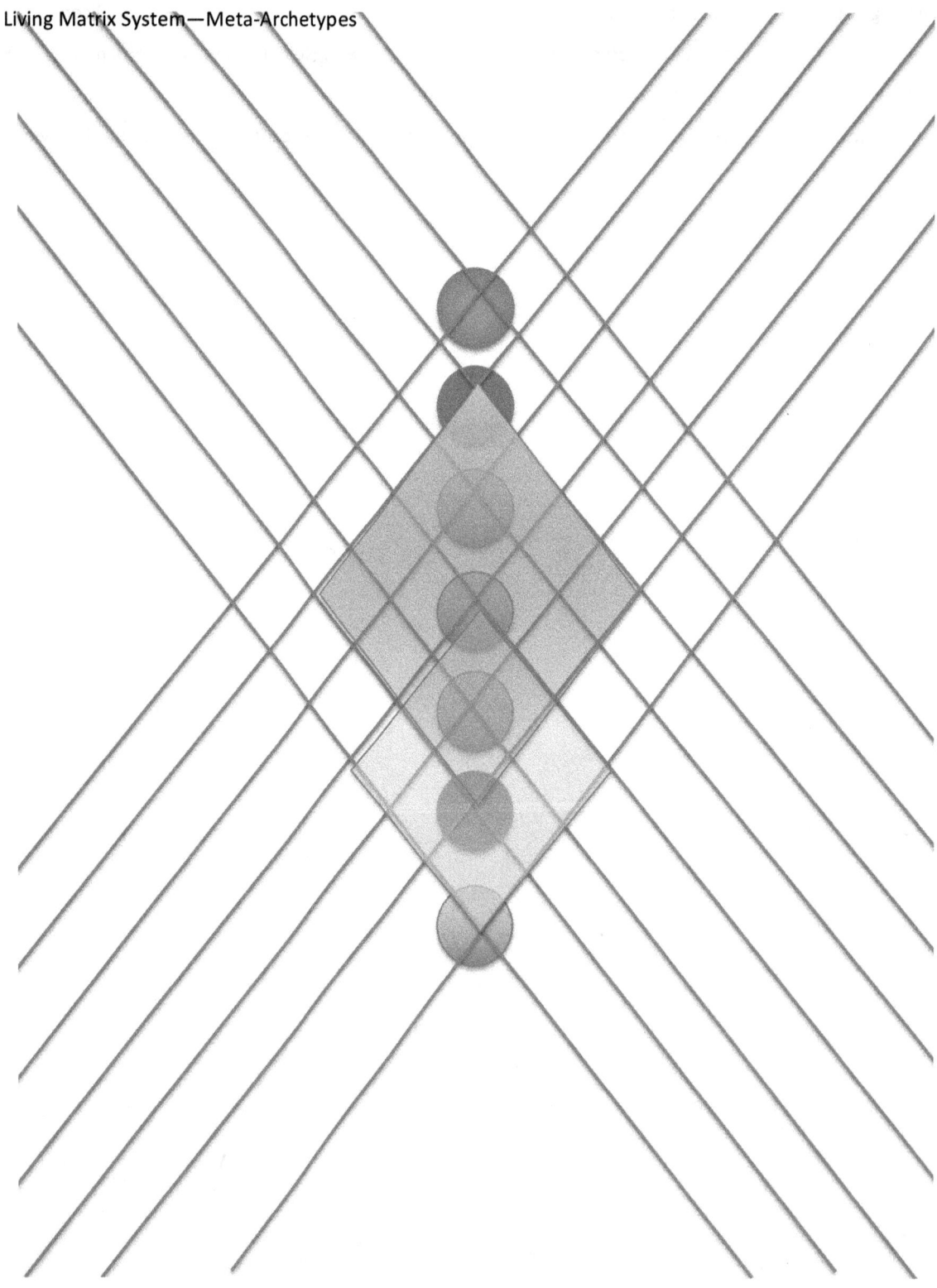

Living Matrix System – Diamond Ladder & Core Centers

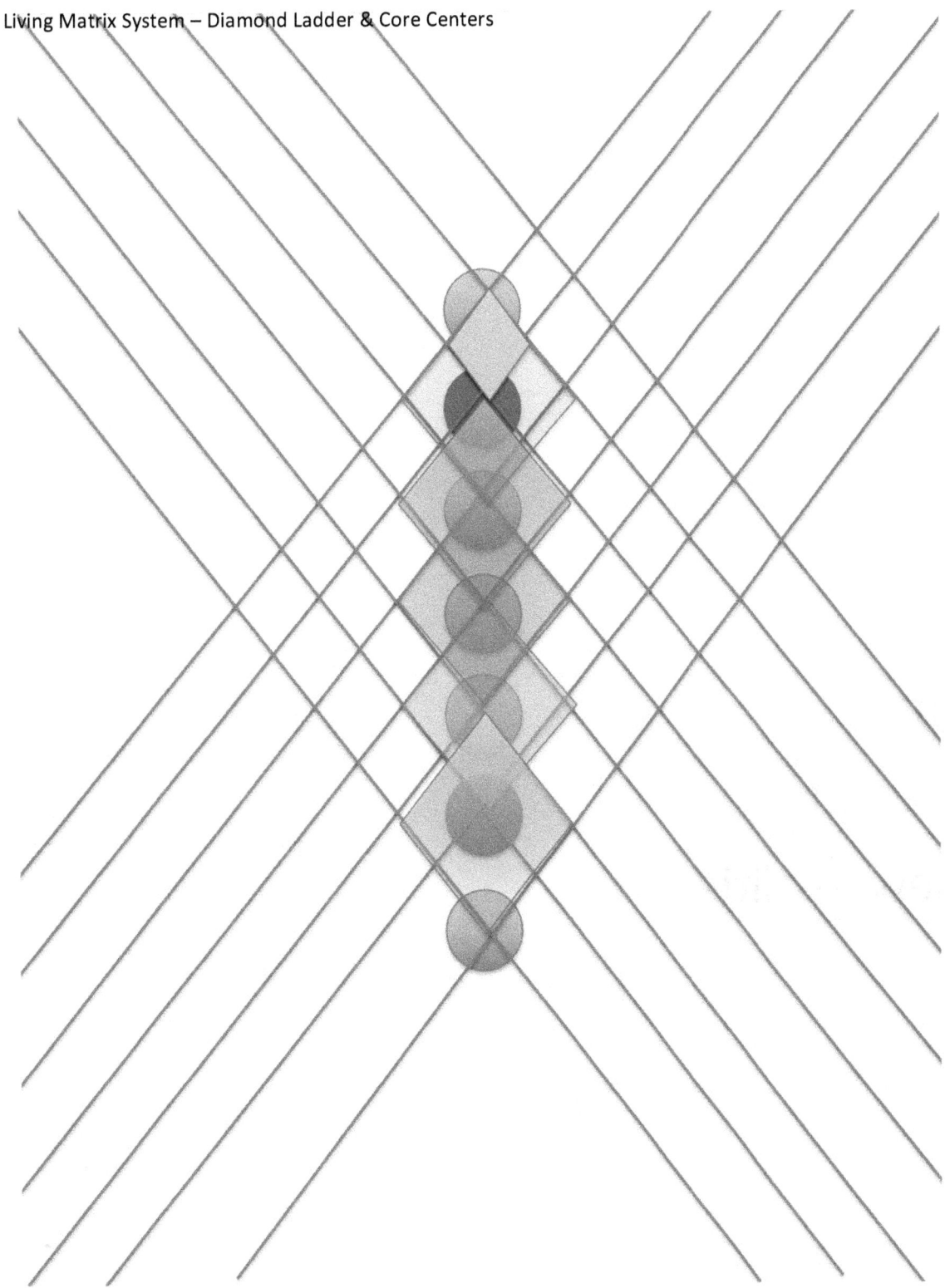

Three
Creating
New Realities

Creating New Realities

Current State:

Date:

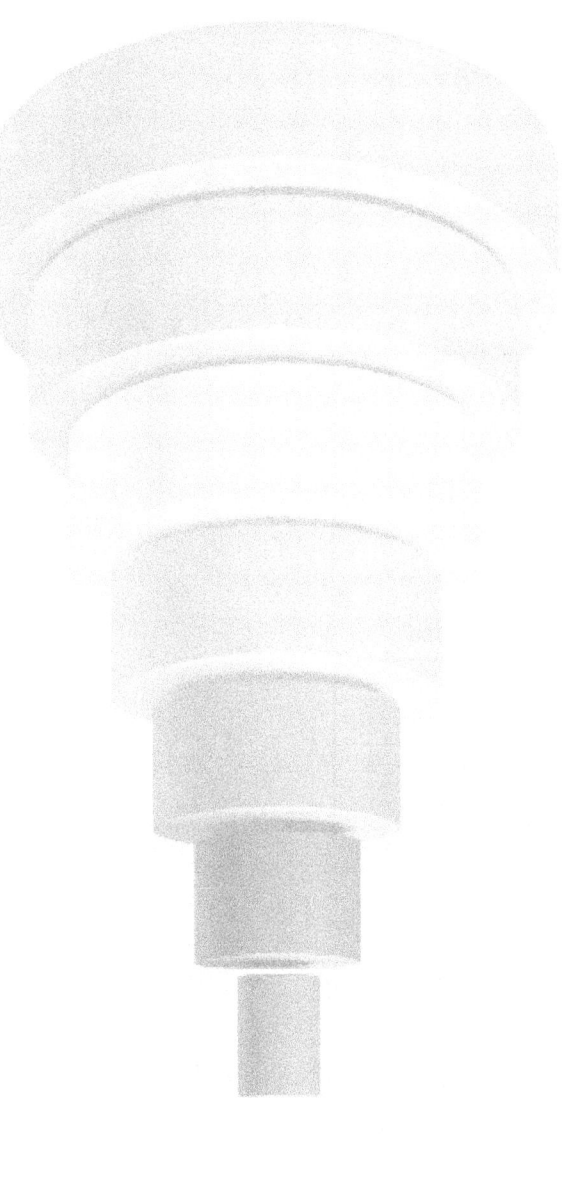

Vibrational Scale 1–1000	Vibration
Enlightenment	700–1000
Peace	600
Joy	540
Love	500
Reason	400
Acceptance	350
Willingness	310
Neutrality	250
Courage	200
Pride	175
Anger	150
Desire	125
Fear	100
Grief	75
Apathy	50
Guilt	30
Shame	20

Source: David R. Hawkins, M.D., Ph.D., Healing & Recovery

Creating New Realities

Desired State:

Date:

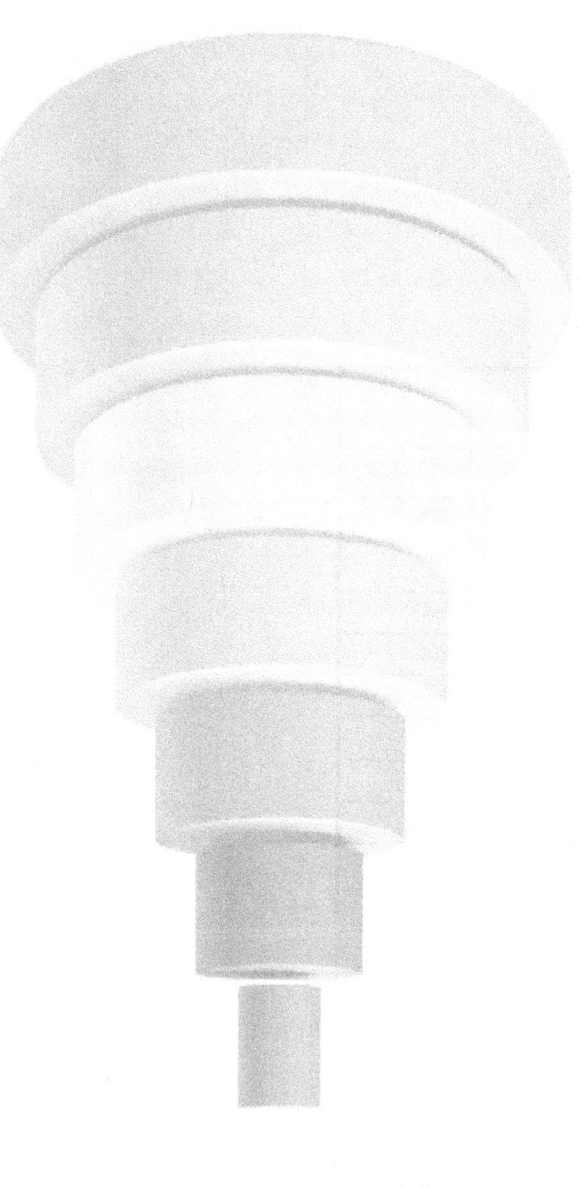

Vibrational Scale 1–1000	Vibration
Enlightenment	700–1000
Peace	600
Joy	540
Love	500
Reason	400
Acceptance	350
Willingness	310
Neutrality	250
Courage	200
Pride	175
Anger	150
Desire	125
Fear	100
Grief	75
Apathy	50
Guilt	30
Shame	20

Source: David R. Hawkins, M.D., Ph.D., Healing & Recovery

Educational Series: Vision Planning

Setting Your Best Intention

_____
_____
_____
_____
_____
_____
_____

Instructions:

Set your best intention by writing it in the present tense as if it has already happened.

Send your intention out into the Universe as far as you can imagine.

Let it go and now walk backwards, keeping your mind's eye on the vision.

Come back to the present with vigil awareness and capture your thoughts, feelings or pain in the body by writing them down.

Be aware of God's co-creation as your vision begins to manifest in the world.

Practice acceptance, gratitude and unconditional love as everyday miracles begin to flow in your life.

Healing & Wellness Beyond Recovery

Intention Statements
Life-Purpose/Career/Job

_____
_____
_____
_____

Family

_____
_____
_____
_____

Health/Well-Being

_____
_____
_____
_____

Self-Care/Self-Love

_____
_____
_____
_____

Relationship

_____
_____
_____
_____

Write Your New Story for the Highest Good

Through the insight attained by picking your archetype characters and the positive intentions you have set, you will be more aware of important shifts changing your life circumstances. This exercise is to establish stable grounding, and serves as a commitment to yourself as you begin to change. It will act as a good reminder of what is really happening. Trust the process and know that everything is in perfect order.

Know that our thoughts have power, and when you reconstruct "who you are" in positive ways in connection with the Universe, you are tapping into an empowered, authentic self.

Remember: do not make major decisions during this passage. When change occurs, it will be natural and flow with ease. If you are resisting, remember to lean into the resistance.

Go ahead. Start writing your new story as if it has already happened, using your archetypes to help tell the story.

Example: My New Story—A Peaceful Loving Relationship

I am in a peaceful loving relationship of oneness and well-being with a man who is above the victim mentality in the space where miracles occur.

As a healer (Meta 2–6) it is my responsibility to promote self-healing, and I am happy to teach the person whom I share my life with these methods for the sake of their own empowerment. I understand life can be messy, and I embrace whatever it may look like in positive ways (Prostitute) without compromising my integrity, spirituality or safety in relationship.

My Divine Child and Mystic have strong knowing capabilities, and it is best I not react in negative ways when adverse intuitive hits present. It is also important I keep my premonitions private to avoid strong holds on the relationship. When I am able to read a situation at an unconscious level, I need to be aware enough to bring this out into the light, and to deal with my relationship at a conscious level, instead of working underneath, where the person is asleep. In my relationship, I have the ability to keep it interesting (Alchemist) using my creativity and intuition to enhance its growth and development.

I have the gift of Exorcist (3rd–5th) and I am aware when negative energies are ready to be released from a person's body. In my past relationships, partners have had resistance and have held back from releasing negative energies for fear of losing themselves, dying to themselves, or the feminine annihilation of the ego. I need to examine myself closer in this area to ascertain why I have kept repeating this pattern. I have pushed myself very hard to grow, and the limiting belief would be, "I am too advanced, and I fear enlightenment will separate me from being connected in relationship." This is false, and I need to get rid of this limiting belief. I need to ask myself, "What am I resisting? Is the intention of my growth a form of running away from my partner?"

I understand there is an unseen presence with a strong influence of love (Lover) and Christ consciousness in my life. In relationship, it is my wish that I am with someone who understands these concepts, and who accepts me as I accept him. I must practice surrendering the relationship to God in order for healing to take place.

I am a Teacher and a Visionary. In my relationship, it is important that I share this space in equal partnership, yet with distinct roles, for the highest good. It is important I do not get ahead of God when given a strong vision, or sabotage that vision out of pride, self-righteousness or frustration.

I am a Storyteller and "story" is key to achieving healing and wellness. I love to write and to express myself in creative ways that enhance the world. I will write Spaces of Love for healing relationships as my next project.

Write Your New Story for the Highest Good

Generational Healing:

Once you identify particular themes in your life that have led you down a path of emotional, spiritual and/or physical destruction, you will start to understand that these patterns are learned behaviors, passed down from seven generations ago.

It takes only a small kernel of awareness to gain strength, courage and willingness with God's grace to change the course of our lives, and to come up into the sweetening spiral of wellness. As you change, you also have the power to influence and change your entire family's energy system.

1. Identify the Big Story (Archetype/Universal Story/Generational Story): Find the truth of the story or archetype theme, as this story has been written in the stars and passed down from generation to generation.

_____
_____
_____

2. Identify the small kernel of truth inside of you (My Story/Core Hurt).

_____
_____
_____

3. Identify where this story is in your body.

_____
_____
_____

4. Create Positive Generational Statements.

_____
_____
_____

Generational Healing Example

1. Identify the Big Story (Archetype/Universal Story/Generational Story): Find the truth of the story or archetype theme, as this story has been written in the stars and passed down from generation to generation.

When we buy into dysfunction or believe people who possess dysfunctional behaviors, this naturally lowers our self-esteem. Dysfunction wants to tell us lies about who we are and turn us away from love, because dysfunctional people fear losing love.

2. Identify the small kernel of truth inside of you (My Story/Core Hurt).

Dysfunctional behaviors bring out the "victim" and make me fearful of being rejected and abandoned. They make me crave or act addicted to love, because dysfunction withholds deeper aspects of love out of fear of annihilation—i.e., grandfather, father, ex-husband or significant other. Therefore, I become a co-addict in the cycle of love/sex addiction.

3. Identify where this story is in your body: Energy Centers 1, 2, 3, 5, 6 (includes victim, healer, prostitute, mystic, divine child, lover)

4. Creating Positive Generational Statements

I believe I am lovable and worthy of truly loving and being loved in many ways, and I accept myself wholly and completely and unconditionally…

I believe my significant other/spouse is worthy of truly loving and being loved in many ways…

I believe my mother, father and grandparents were lovable and worthy of truly loving and being loved in many ways…

I believe my children and their future children are lovable and worthy of truly loving and being loved in many ways…

Write Your New Family Story for the Highest Good

Vision Tracking

Positive Flow: What is coming in on my wish list? What do I need to lean into? What am I grateful for? How am I being supported?

Week 1

Week 2

Week 3

Week 4

Week 5

Week 6

Week 7

Week 8

Vision Tracking

Negative Flow: What is not working? Inner resistance? Outer resistance? What do I need to let go of? Whom do I need to stay away from that makes me feel unsupported?

Week 1

Week 2

Week 3

Week 4

Week 5

Week 6

Week 7

Week 8

Pause.

Take a deep breath.

Breathe out.

You are healing.

Four

Your Vital Energy

Educational Series: Vital & Alive

Your Vital Energy

By learning to access your vital energy system, you are actually tapping into your body's natural healing abilities to restore, rejuvenate, enhance and boost the immune system, autonomic nervous system and endocrine system. The various energy centers, also known as the chakra system, regulate and control many aspects of your life, such as your emotions, self-empowerment and the capacities to love, effectively communicate, increase your intuitive abilities and focus your mind.

From the day you were conceived in your mother's womb, you experienced wonderful and not-so-wonderful life situations that shaped your health, vitality and well-being. With proper knowledge and understanding of how to care for your energy centers, you are more likely to optimize your health and wellness. Here is why: when negative energy enters your body, toxic residue forms. If the residue goes unresolved or un-dissolved, layer upon layer builds up, deeper into the muscle tissues, nerves, bones and liquids in your body. Your body's vital energy flow becomes restricted, or even blocked. You may become physically unhealthy, and you may act out with inappropriate behavior.

With energy awareness, you learn how to manage your vital energy centers and to unblock and direct your energy in positive ways. With new understanding, you will learn to dissolve or change the cycle of negative patterns. As you release negative energy, you will create new space for healthy energy to flow, leading you to higher levels of wellness. As you enhance your vital energy system, you will have an even greater capacity not only to dispel negative energies, but to restore and maintain the health of your vital organs, such as the heart, lungs, liver and kidneys. You may actually notice you have more energy, and can enjoy life to its fullest

Your Energy Centers

In the field of Energy Medicine, trained professionals work with what is called the life-force, vital energy, Chi, Qi, or the Holy Spirit, in order to create or empower their clients' wellness. As vital energy moves through your system's pathway, activation occurs in several energy centers located at different points, or what acupuncturists call meridians, around your body.

There are seven major energy centers running seven layers deep in the body. They range anywhere from eight to ten inches in diameter. Determining the health, vitality and well-being of each center is similar to rating the quality of a diamond. A trained medical intuitive has the ability to see your energy centers and to determine their clarity, color, size and even geometrical patterns in relation to your emotional, spiritual and physical origins. Viewed from the outside in, the anatomy of a center resembles a pinwheel spinning inside a cylinder with healthy energy flowing clockwise.

These energy centers oscillate at various speeds, or frequencies, depending on the quality of your health and well-being. They intricately connect and stimulate each gland within the endocrine system. These centers are like little universes unto themselves, synthesizing incredible amounts of knowledge to help regulate the state of your emotional, spiritual and physical body. Each universe, or energy center, contains the blueprint of energy patterns, or cell memories, working interdependently with the autonomic nervous system and endocrine system as mentioned earlier. By becoming aware and learning how to work with your energy centers as outlined in this workbook, you will come closer to accessing the everyday miracle of staying healthy, vital and well.

Nervous System and Corresponding Energy Centers

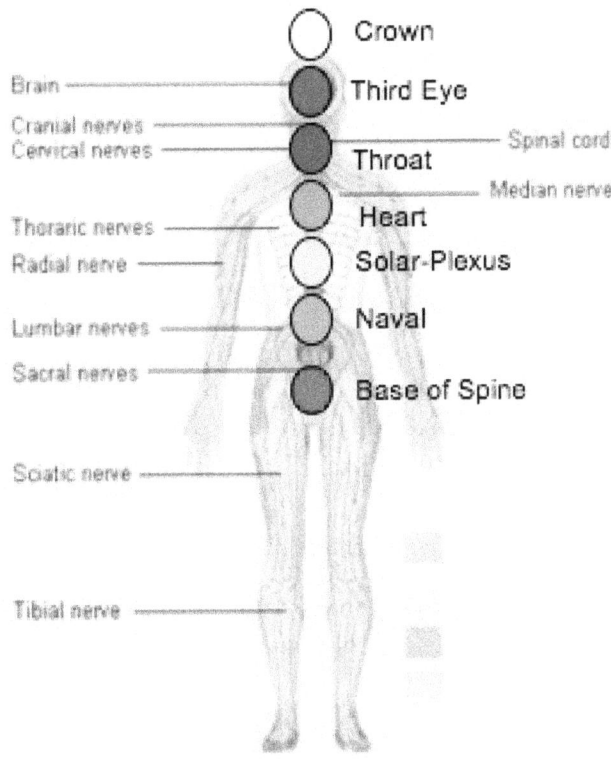

Endocrine System and Energy Center Correspondences

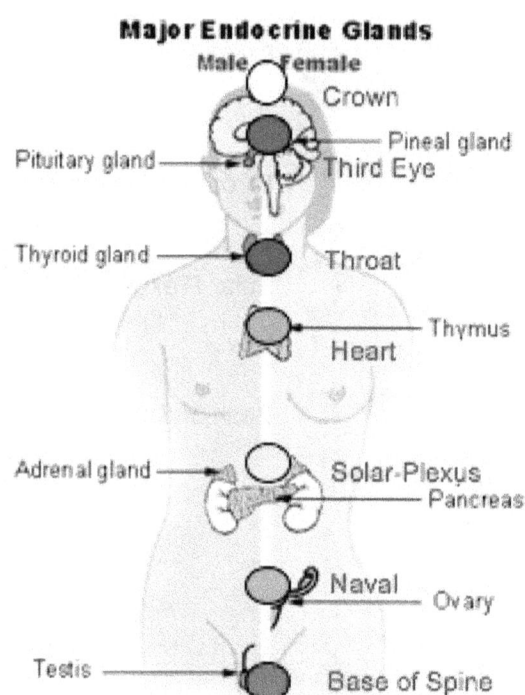

	Body of Wellness. Body of Grace.			
Energy Centers	Life Themes	Organs	Mental/Emotional Issues	Physical Dysfunctions
7	Acceptance of one's life. Capacity to fulfill one's purpose and find meaning in life. Knowingness and spiritual identity. Well-developed sense of self. Strong connection to one's personal spirituality. Clear sense of one's life path. Ability to see the larger picture. Importance of manifesting the spirit in physical reality.	Muscular System. Skeletal System. Skin.	Lack of ability in trusting life. Diminished sense of self. Inability to take control of life. Unwillingness to recognize and connect with the spiritual element of life. Sense of not wanting to be a part of life, i.e., not feeling that one belongs here.	Energetic Disorders. Mystical Depression. Chronic exhaustion that is not linked to a physical disorder. Extreme sensitivities to light, sound and other environmental factors.
Energy Centers	Life Themes	Organs	Mental/Emotional Issues	Physical Dysfunctions
6	The center of clairvoyance and intuition. Helps maintain balance between intuition and analytical thought. Allows one to see the truth in situations. An openness to other people's ideas. Use of knowledge, higher reasoning and intuitive skills.	Nervous system and brain. Pineal gland, hypothalamus, pituitary gland. Eyes, ears and nose.	Dogmatic, judgmental thinking. Over-reliance on logic and analytical thought. Inability to see the truth in people or situations. Feelings of inadequacy. Inability to learn from experience.	Brain tumor, hemorrhage, stroke and neurological disturbances. Blindness and deafness. Full spinal difficulties. Learning disabilities and seizures.
Energy Centers	Life Themes	Organs	Mental/Emotional Issues	Physical Dysfunctions
5	Development of *will* power. God's *will*. Creative expression and communication. Manifestation of the *will* in the physical form.	Mouth, teeth and gums. Pharynx, trachea, esophagus. Thyroid and parathyroid. Neck and cervical vertebrae.	Fear of expression. Inability to speak your *truth*. Inability to bring your *will* forward in the world. Unwillingness to recognize and utilize your creativity.	Addiction and eating disorders.

Energy Centers	Life Themes	Organs	Mental/Emotional Issues	Physical Dysfunctions
4	All issues concerning love and compassion, including creating from the heart, following your heart's desire, love of other forms of life. Balance between caring for yourself and others.	Heart and circulatory system. Breast, lungs, ribs, diaphragm. Thymus gland. Mid-back, chest muscles, arms, shoulders. Upper thoracic vertebrae.	Inability to feel or express love for self or others. Feelings of loss and grief. Anger, hatred, resentment, self-centeredness. Inability to forgive.	Congestive heart failure. Myocardial infarction (heart attack). Asthma, lung cancer and pneumonia. Upper back and shoulder problems. Breast cancer.

Energy Centers	Life Themes	Organs	Mental/Emotional Issues	Physical Dysfunctions
3	Personal power, fear of intimidation and rejection, lack of self-esteem and survival intuitions.	Stomach, spleen, pancreas, liver, gallbladder, adrenals. Lower thoracic spine.	Power struggles and associated anger. Low self-esteem, low self-confidence and low self-respect. Excessive generalized fear and difficulty making decisions. Hypersensitivity to criticism.	Gastric ulcers, pancreatitis and diabetes. Indigestion, chronic or acute anorexia or bulimia, liver dysfunction, hepatitis, adrenal dysfunction, mid-back pain. Lethargy and morning fatigue.

Energy Centers	Life Themes	Organs	Mental/Emotional Issues	Physical Dysfunctions
2	Power and control in the material world. Money, sex and control of other people.	Reproductive organs. Large intestine (including appendix), small intestine. Kidney and bladder. Lower lumbar vertebrae.	Blame and guilt. Sex, relationship and money. Ethics and honor in the relationship. Mood swings, depression. Overwhelming feelings of empathy. Inability to express emotions in a healthy way.	Chronic lower back pain, sciatica. Large and small intestines. Reproductive organs. Urinary system. Appendix and lower lumbar vertebra. OB/GYN issues and sexual dysfunction. Gastrointestinal issues including constipation, diarrhea and gas. Chronic low back pain, sciatica, urinary problems. Lack of creativity. Inability to have positive sexual relationship.

Energy Centers	Life Themes	Organs	Mental/Emotional Issues	Physical Dysfunctions
1	Safety in the physical world.	Physical body support (grounding). Base of spine. Legs, hip joints, bones, feet, rectum. Immune system.	Physical family and group safety and security. Ability to provide for life's necessities. Ability to stand up for self. Feeling at home. Anxiety, stress, emotional and economic poverty beliefs. Social and familial law and order.	Chronic lower back pain. Sciatica, varicose veins. Rectal tumors, cancer, depression and immune-related disorders.

Pause.

Take a deep breath.

Breathe out.

You are healing.

Five

Core Healing

This is where we learn to fly.

Educational Series: Presence for Protection

Creating a Safe Place

It is important to create a safe place when we enter into healing ourselves. Make sure you are comfortable and ask for protection using one of the below methods. If you feel more comfortable using one of your own prayers of protection, feel free to use that one instead.

Gratitude, Praise and Guidance

Start with prayers of gratitude, thanking your Creator, God/Jesus, or the Universe for all the beautiful wonders of your life. Bless your children, your relationship and lessons learned. Thank God/Jesus for peace, love, joy and happiness each day, regardless of any negative surroundings. Finally, ask for guidance and keep your ears close to your heart to hear what it is whispering to you.

Merging with the Divine

Visualize a violet energy coming in through your crown and allow the energy to flow down through the center of your body, passing from head to toe. Continue the flow down into the earth and securely fasten yourself. Expand the beam of light from your center into every cell of your body and into your auric field, about four or eight feet in circumference.

Heart Tapping

By gently tapping on your 4th center for two to three minutes each day, you can create healthy boundaries to protect yourself from negative energies entering your field. In many cases, this can also help dislodge or release negative emotions such as anger, resentment, sadness and shame.

White Light of Christ

For added protection, imagine the white light of Christ bursting from your heart center. Allow the white light to fill your 4th energy center, and expand it into your body by filling each and every cell in your body. Visualize beyond your body and form a protective bubble ranging from six to eight feet in diameter, with three feet under the earth and three feet above.

Umbrella of Grace

Spirituality/Personal Growth
- Twelve Steps
- Meditation
- Prayer
- Self-Help
- Service
- Storytelling
- Talk Therapy

Life Purpose Wellness

Healing
- Body Work
- Energy Therapy
- Archetypes
- Positive Affirmations
- Visualization
- Healing Touch
- Essential Oils
- Yoga

Loving Spirit

Courage Worksheet	Event & Cause of Event	How did it make you feel?	Inner-Child Reaction. How old is your child?	Energy Centers Pain/Illness	Archetypes, light and dark aspects

Pride Worksheet	Event & Cause of Event	How did it make you feel?	Inner-Child Reaction. How old is your child?	Energy Centers Pain/Illness	Archetypes, light and dark aspects

Anger Worksheet	Event & Cause of Event	How did it make you feel?	Inner-Child Reaction. How old is your child?	Energy Centers Pain/Illness	Archetypes, light and dark aspects

Desire Worksheet	Event & Cause of Event	How did it make you feel?	Inner-Child Reaction. How old is your child?	Energy Centers Pain/Illness	Archetypes, light and dark aspects

Fear Worksheet	Event & Cause of Event	How did it make you feel?	Inner-Child Reaction. How old is your child?	Energy Centers Pain/Illness	Archetypes, light and dark aspects

Healing & Wellness Beyond Recovery

Grief Worksheet	Event & Cause of Event	How did it make you feel?	Inner-Child Reaction. How old is your child?	Energy Centers Pain/Illness	Archetypes, light and dark aspects

Apathy Worksheet	Event & Cause of Event	How did it make you feel?	Inner-Child Reaction. How old is your child?	Energy Centers Pain/Illness	Archetypes, light and dark aspects

Guilt Worksheet	Event & Cause of Event	How did it make you feel?	Inner-Child Reaction. How old is your child?	Energy Centers Pain/Illness	Archetypes, light and dark aspects

Healing & Wellness Beyond Recovery

Shame Worksheet	Event & Cause of Event	How did it make you feel?	Inner-Child Reaction. How old is your child?	Energy Centers Pain/Illness	Archetypes, light and dark aspects

Pause.

Take a deep breath.

Breathe out.

You are healing.

Undoing Phase

What appears to be more crisis really isn't. It is an undoing phase. Be prepared for things to look worse before they get better. Make no major decisions while in mid-stream. Everything has to be un-done in order to be made right according to the grace of God's will. When you surrender to the process and turn your life over to the will of God, know that everything has already been taken care of. Make sure you get out of the way, as you are going through a transformation for the new you to emerge. Know that your truth has been declared to the Universe. Everything will be corrected. There is nothing you have to do other than to take note that the Universe is conspiring for your greatest good. From this point on, everything is merely a correction. Know that when you have this type of awareness, all is in the best interest of your personal well-being, no matter what unfortunate circumstances occur. Have presence of mind to see the change inside of yourself and around you as it is happening. Try not to make decisions before the best decision becomes obvious. If someone else is making decisions for you, trust they are using inner guidance. If not, know that these decisions may prove to carry no weight in the future. Trust that you are being cared for, as these decisions are coming from a power greater than yourself. There is great power in this process. Everything will begin to change. Expect change to come even in the form of good pain or illness, because the stress you have been carrying has to come out of your body at some point.

Resistance

Until you accept the very thing you are resisting, everything remains unchanged, out of sorts or in chaos. When you surrender to the process and move past your fears, there is sweetness on the other side. You may say to yourself, "If I give in to this situation, I am going to be miserable. I fear it's going to make my life worse than what I am already experiencing." For example, when I had the inner prompting to start The Dove House, I said, "No way" because I had recently let go of a failing business and had just come off a two-year family crisis. I was financially and emotionally drained. There was "no way" I was going to start something new—but eventually I had no choice. I had to give in to what was persisting inside of me. After three days of creating The Dove House, I was surprised to see it was my heart's desire. It was everything I ever wanted—yet why was there resistance? I asked of God, "Please, I cannot lead this. You have to show me the way. Otherwise, I will fail." God has kept His promise, and it has been amazing to witness each day as The Dove House spreads its wings.

I can recall countless other times when I have had to give in to my resistance, and each time, it has felt dreadful prior to the surrender—like a small death. In fact, it *is* a small death. It is the death of the ego. I would say to myself, "I can't believe I have to do the very thing I do not want to do." But each time I gave in and pushed past my fear, miracles resulted.

It can work the same way with healing past trauma in your life. There seems to be this same type of resistance to healing the very thing that needs to heal. We push back. Our saboteur comes out, because it is hard to face something that is so painful inside of us. Yet if we choose to continue to ignore what persists, the same patterns will continue to present themselves in our relationships, finances and career, etc., as they wreak havoc in our lives.

Blueprint for Change

Next, be aware of who is showing up in your life. They might be very sick people attracted to you pushing your weakest buttons or causing you pain where you hurt the most. There may also be incredible people coming to you, fulfilling your heart's deepest desires, but they may trigger other sources of pain inside you as well. Everyone is a blueprint of different aspects of you asking to heal. What is most important is to surround yourself with people who are supportive, honest, trustworthy, truthful, loving and committed to something greater. They are on the same journey as you, and there is no need to push them down or away, or to be in competition with them. It is not about where you are in relationship to where they are. In fact, you can spiral down at anytime if you lose sight of who you are and where you are in the process. Stay focused on reaching upwards into healing and wellness levels of consciousness for the greatest good in the world.

Key words to remember: Awareness, Surrender, Cooperation

Six

Energy Strategies

Energy Strategies

Clearing & Cleansing Centers—*Good for relieving depression or taking on other people's feelings*

Cleansing your energy centers is as important as brushing your teeth each day. You can do this simple exercise while taking a shower: Starting with your first center, located at the base of your spine, cleanse each energy center until you reach your crown chakra. Spin each center counterclockwise four times. After completing sets of four, flick the toxic energy down the drain. Before proceeding to the next energy center, spin clockwise one time and pull an imaginary string outward for center alignment. Wash your hands with soap between each cleansing.

Interlocking Fingers

To balance after cleansing, conclude by interlocking fingers together, with thumbs side-by-side in an upright position. This prayerful position will bring balance into your system in a matter of minutes.

Head & Heart Meditation—*Good for relieving depression, addiction, despair*

In a supine (lying down) position, place one hand on your heart and the other over your forehead. Be silent for at least five to ten minutes, while you fill your diaphragm with oxygen and breathe out slowly to relax your mind and body. Next, use your fingers, as if they were a comb, and swipe the energy away from your body in a counterclockwise motion at least four times. At the end of each set, take the dirty energy between your fingers and flick it away from your body. Repeat this exercise at least three times and remember to wash your hands when finished. It is also recommended you journal your thoughts, before or after, for additional clearing of mind and heart.

Correcting Energetic Reversal

Repeat each statement one to three times while tapping or rubbing the points located directly above the breasts.

"Even though I don't want to heal/change/live my soul's purpose in _____, I absolutely love, honor and respect myself."

"Even though I don't deserve to heal/change/live my soul's purpose in _____, I absolutely love, honor and respect myself."

"Even though I don't feel like it's safe to heal/change/live my soul's purpose in _____, I absolutely love, honor and respect myself."

"Even though I don't deserve to heal/change/live my soul's purpose in _____, I absolutely love, honor and respect myself."

"Even though I don't believe I will heal/change/live my soul's purpose in _____, I absolutely love, honor and respect myself."

Tapping Method Instructions for WHEE: Whole Health—Easily and Effectively®

WHEE is a self-healing method for anxiety, depression, pain and stress relief. It is easily learned, easy to use, and users report it can provide rapid and deep relief.

The practice of WHEE involves four steps:
1. Identify a feeling or thought we would like to change.
Focus on a physical pain or a single incident that has left a negative feeling. Assess how strong a feeling this is on a scale of 0–10 (where 0 = doesn't bother me at all, and 10 = worst I could possibly feel). This is called **SUDS** (Subjective Units of Distress Scale).

2. Alternately stimulate the right and left side of the body.
Examples: move the eyes repeatedly, back and forth from right to left; alternately, tap the right and left eyebrow at the point nearest the nose; pat the biceps of each arm (a "butterfly hug"); or any other rhythmic, repeated alternate right and left stimulation.

3. Recite a counteracting affirmation.
Here is a generic counteracting affirmation, adapted from EFT:
"Even though I have this [pain, anxiety, panic, fear, etc.—be specific when filling in the blank], I love and accept myself wholly and completely, and [God/Christ/Allah/the Infinite Source] loves and accepts me wholly and completely and unconditionally." [If any of this does not feel comfortable, we use whatever strong counteracting positive affirmation suits us best at the time we need it.] After tapping for a few minutes, check your level of distress by using the SUDS again. It will usually decrease. Repeat the assessing and tapping until it is at zero.

4. Install a replacement or positive affirmation.
Example: I feel less stressed/painful/anxious. Prior to starting the installation of the replacement affirmation, assess the strength of the statement and feelings of the problem statement on a scale of 0–10, where 0 = "I don't believe this at all," and 10 = "I believe this statement as strongly as I possibly can." Working on your issues when you are not under stress is highly recommended *before* you work on them in stressful situations.
Copyright © 2008 Daniel J. Benor, MD. All rights reserved.

Educational Series: Emotional Well-Being

Assessing Your Feelings

Write down a feeling question:
_____
_____
_____

Next, ask yourself this question while holding your hand on each energy center until you receive an answer. Write down each answer you receive for each energy center. Sometimes there are no answers, in which case you may leave it blank.

7th Spirituality
_____

6th Intuition
_____

5th God's Will/Your Will
_____

4th Matters of the Heart
_____

3rd Self-Empowerment
_____

2nd Sex, Money and Relationship
_____

1st Safety in the World
_____

Educational Series: Pain: Your Opportunity to Heal

Apply the WHEE Method for each energy center that holds a negative feeling.
Create a counteracting statement involving thoughts, feelings or pain in the body. Once you have constructed the statement, identify the core hurt and what it reminds you of from your past hurts. Allow images to come up, and use them as clues surfacing from your unconscious self for healing to occur.

Energy Center: **Pain:**   **Archetype:**

Counteracting Statement:

Even though i.e., I am resentful....I am angry... I have a sore shoulder... My heart hurts...

_____
_____
_____
_____
_____
_____
_____

Deeper Core Hurt...and it reminds me of i.e., when I felt rejected, abandoned, shameful or guilty

_____
_____
_____
_____
_____

—I love and accept myself wholly and completely, and [God/Christ/Allah/the Infinite Source] loves and accepts me wholly and completely and unconditionally."

SUDS Rating: _____/_____/_____/_____/_____

Healing & Wellness Beyond Recovery

Positive Statement

I am
_____
_____
_____
_____
_____
_____

—and I love and accept myself wholly and completely, and [God/Christ/Allah/the Infinite Source] loves and accepts me wholly and completely and unconditionally."

SUDS Rating: _____/_____/_____/_____/_____

Healing & Wellness Beyond Recovery

Energy Center: **Pain:**   **Archetype:**

Counteracting Statement:

Even though

_____
_____
_____
_____
_____
_____
_____

and it reminds me of

_____
_____
_____
_____
_____
_____

—I love and accept myself wholly and completely, and [God/Christ/Allah/the Infinite Source] loves and accepts me wholly and completely and unconditionally."

SUDS Rating: _____/_____/_____/_____/_____

Healing & Wellness Beyond Recovery

Positive Statement

I am
_____
_____
_____
_____
_____
_____

—and I love and accept myself wholly and completely, and [God/Christ/Allah/the Infinite Source] loves and accepts me wholly and completely and unconditionally."

SUDS Rating: _____/_____/_____/_____/_____

Healing & Wellness Beyond Recovery

Energy Center: **Pain:**   **Archetype:**

Counteracting Statement:

Even though

_____
_____
_____
_____
_____
_____
_____

and it reminds me of

_____
_____
_____
_____
_____
_____

—I love and accept myself wholly and completely, and [God/Christ/Allah/the Infinite Source] loves and accepts me wholly and completely and unconditionally."

SUDS Rating: _____/_____/_____/_____/_____

Positive Statement

I am

_____
_____
_____
_____
_____
_____
_____
_____

—and I love and accept myself wholly and completely, and [God/Christ/Allah/the Infinite Source] loves and accepts me wholly and completely and unconditionally."

SUDS Rating: _____/_____/_____/_____/_____

Energy Center: **Pain:**   **Archetype:**

Counteracting Statement:

Even though

_____
_____
_____
_____
_____
_____

and it reminds me of

_____
_____
_____
_____
_____
_____

— I love and accept myself wholly and completely, and [God/Christ/Allah/the Infinite Source] loves and accepts me wholly and completely and unconditionally."

SUDS Rating: _____/_____/_____/_____/_____

Positive Statement

I am

_____
_____
_____
_____
_____
_____
_____
_____

—and I love and accept myself wholly and completely, and [God/Christ/Allah/the Infinite Source] loves and accepts me wholly and completely and unconditionally."

SUDS Rating: _____/_____/_____/_____/_____

Healing & Wellness Beyond Recovery

Energy Center: **Pain:**   **Archetype:**

Counteracting Statement:

Even though

_____
_____
_____
_____
_____
_____

and it reminds me of

_____
_____
_____
_____
_____
_____

—I love and accept myself wholly and completely, and [God/Christ/Allah/the Infinite Source] loves and accepts me wholly and completely and unconditionally."

SUDS Rating: _____/_____/_____/_____/_____

Positive Statement

I am

_____
_____
_____
_____
_____
_____
_____
_____

—and I love and accept myself wholly and completely, and [God/Christ/Allah/the Infinite Source] loves and accepts me wholly and completely and unconditionally."

SUDS Rating: _____/_____/_____/_____/_____

Pause.

Take a deep breath.

Breathe out.

You are healing.

Healing & Wellness Beyond Recovery

Seven
Amends & Forgiveness

For most people, forgiveness does not come easy—especially when they were the ones who were hurt. If you ask someone to forgive, right away he says, "They don't deserve forgiveness." When you've been abused or victimized, the last thing in the world you can imagine is letting the perpetrator off the hook. The term "hook," literally taken, gives rise to an image of an angular, metal object "hooked" into something; and if that something is a living creature, it probably hurts. In other words, the inability to forgive keeps you connected to pain—your pain and the other person's pain. When you forgive, you release pain and the healing graces pour into you twofold.

To *forgive* is to pardon or be pardoned from harboring ill feelings such as resentment, anger, confusion, shame, guilt or heartache against someone or yourself. *Forgiveness* improves health and well-being. Studies show that people who forgive are happier and healthier than those who hold resentments [1]. The first study to look at how forgiveness improves physical health discovered that, when people think about forgiving an offender, it leads to improved functioning in their cardiovascular and nervous systems [2].

A study at the University of Wisconsin found that the more forgiving people were, the less they suffered from a wide range of illnesses. The less-forgiving people reported a greater number of health problems [3]. A longitudinal study conducted by Dr. Robert Enright from the University of Wisconsin–Madison focused on what kind of person is more likely to be forgiving. People who were generally more neurotic, angry and hostile in life were less likely to forgive another person, even after a long time had passed. Specifically, these people were more likely to continue to avoid their transgressors, and to want to enact revenge upon them two-and-a-half years after the transgression [4].

The research of Dr. Fred Luskin of Stanford University shows that forgiveness can be learned. Dr. Luskin's work is based on seven major research projects concerning the effects of forgiveness, giving empirical validity to the concept that forgiveness is not only powerful but also excellent for your health. Dr. Fred Luskin is the author of the book, *Learning to Forgive* (http://learningtoforgive.com/). He was presented with a Champion of Forgiveness award by the Forgiveness Alliance ([5]) for his groundbreaking work with forgiveness, reconciliation and peace.

Source: http://en.wikipedia.org/wiki/Forgiveness#Research (reference notes are included in the bibliography section at end of article).

Forgiveness Inventory Checklist

Forgiveness Inventory	Release Resent	Release Heartache	Release Anger	Release Shame	Release Guilt	Release Grudge	Release Jealousy	Release Desire	Release Fear	Release Grief
Mother										
Father										
Brother(s)										
Sister(s)										
Children										
Spouse/Ex										
In-Laws										
Past Relationships										
Friends										
Business Associate										
Community										
God/Higher Power										
Self										

Eight
Affirmations,
Gifts & Gratitude

Collecting Your Positive Statements

1.

2.

3.

4.

5.

6.

7.

8.

9.

10.

Acknowledging Your Gifts

1.

2.

3.

4.

5.

6.

7.

8.

9.

10.

Thanks and Gratitude for Miracles

Give thanks and gratitude for the miracles you have received since you began *Healing & Wellness Beyond Recovery*:

_____
_____
_____
_____
_____
_____
_____
_____
_____
_____
_____
_____
_____

Pause.

Take a deep breath.

Breathe out.

You are healing.

Appendix: Educational Series

Vision Planning

Vital & Alive

Presence for Protection

Trauma & Emotional Well-Being

Pain: Your Opportunity to Heal

Vision Planning
To Achieve Your Highest Good in the World

By Kathleen Riley

Create a Powerful Vision

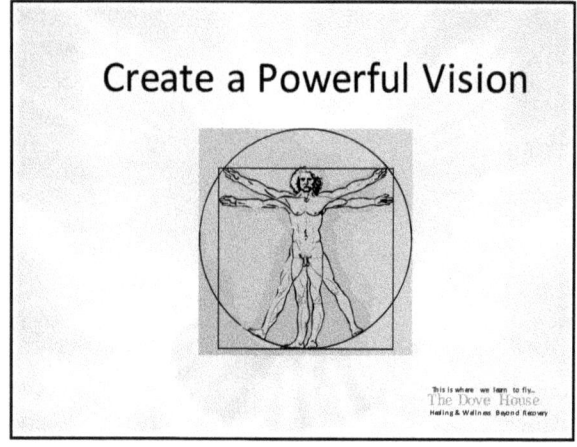

Imagine a Sweetening Spiral

- Consciously reverse your direction and move up the spiral
- Create new realities and new improved life themes
- Get into the flow of well-being
- Create positive thoughts and feelings

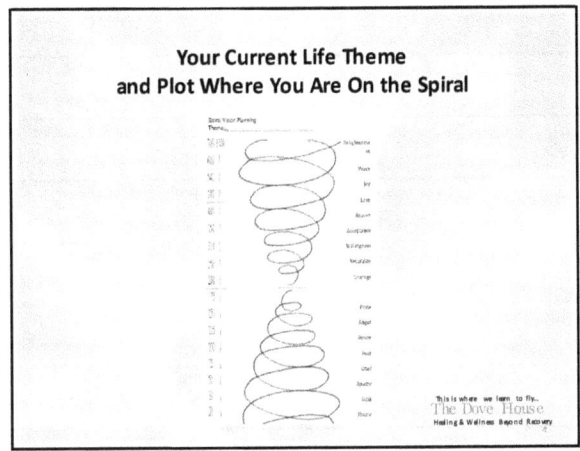

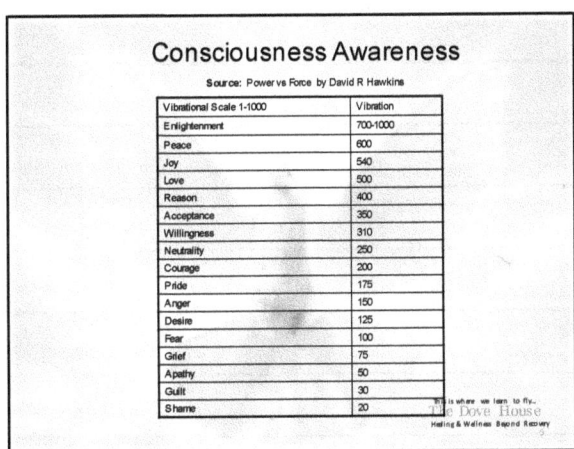

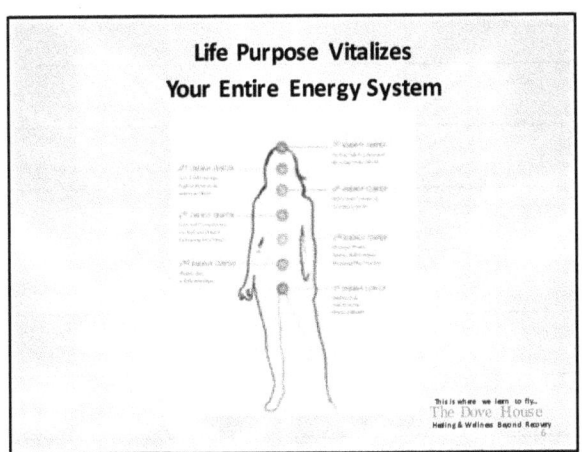

Identify Where You Want to Be

- Where you are on the spiral
- Where you want to be
- What is your life theme(s)
- What is your new life theme(s)
- What have been your reactions
- What are your new actions

Identifying Your Vision

- Determine the areas you wish to improve, i.e. family, relationship, finances, etc. over the course of a year.
- Create a visual snap shot of what you look like and how you feel, i.e. create a vision board.
- Determine the type of environment and the people who support your wellness vision

Characteristics of a Vision Statement

- Optimal future state – the mental picture – of what you want to achieve over time.
- Provides guidance and inspiration as to what you'd focus on achieving in five, ten, or more years.
- Functions as the 'north star'.
- Written in an inspirational manner and in the present tense.

Creating Your Vision

- Written in the present tense and in an inspirational manner
- Add a phrase that recognizes a power greater than yourself
  - "... or something better."
  - "... according to my heart's desire as God knows me best."
  - "...and for the greatest good."

EXPECT MIRACLES
(As If They've Already Happened)

Positive Vision Statement:
(Write it in the present tense)

_____
_____
_____
_____

Imagine A New Life Theme
Plot Where You Want to Be On the Spiral

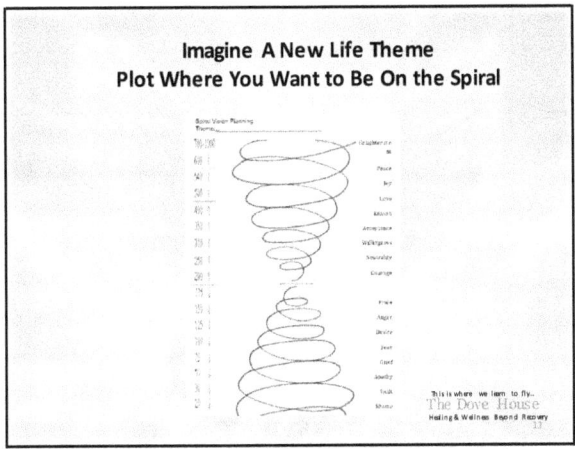

Taking Ownership

- Step into the energy you are creating
- Shift into actions of being and doing
- Let go of outcomes
- Align yourself closer to who shares your vision, i.e. social activities, volunteer positions, new friends, spiritual community, church, health club, sporting activities

To Let Go

To Let Go is not to stop caring;
it is recognizing I can't do it for someone else.

To Let Go is not to cut myself off;
it is realizing I can't control another.

To Let Go is not to enable, but to allow learning from natural consequences.

To Let Go is not to fight powerlessness, but to accept the outcome is not always in my hands.

To Let Go is not to try to change or blame others;
it's to make the most of myself.

To Let Go is not to care for, but to care about.

To Let Go is not to fix;
it's to be supportive.

To Let Go is not to judge;
it's to allow another to be a human being.

To Let Go is not to try to arrange outcomes, but to allow others to affect their own destinies.

To Let Go is not to be protective;
it's to permit another to face their own reality.

To Let Go is not to regulate anyone, but to strive to become what I dream to be.

Celebrate In the NOW

- Very important to be present to the energy flow as you walk backwards and keep your eyes fixed on the vision
- Be aware of what's coming in and how decisions are being made.
- Stay in touch with your momentum in the NOW for generating more flow.
- Make sure you are aligned with an environment of support.

Create Space to Welcome in Change

Simple Action Steps

Focus
Begin by sitting up straight in your favorite chair, in a quiet room.

Heart Center
Now shift your energy from your head into your heart. Breathe in and out from your heart for a few minutes until you are relaxed. Ask yourself, "What is my truth about ...? What is really going on with...?"

Solar-plexus
Next, imagine bringing your energy further down to your solar-plexus located below your heart and ask yourself, "Is something getting in my way? What are my barriers? What are my obstacles? What am I really afraid of? Can I let go?

Taking Inventory

Everyday Miracles

Step 3 – Personal Inventory

Next, imagine bringing your energy further down into your solar-plexus which is located eight inches below your heart.

Ask yourself:
- "Is something getting in my way?"
- "What are my barriers?"
- "What are my obstacles?"
- "What am I really afraid of?"
- "Can I let go?"

Take note of the images or thoughts that come up. Don't push them away. Stay focused in your heart. Mentally note what's being presented or coming up first. Write them down in the order as they appear.

If nothing comes up, review your assessment and notice the areas you wish to improve. Repeat the heart-centering exercise and write down the images that appear.

Determining Obstacles

Thoughts	Negative Energy/Obstacles
1.	1.
2.	2.
3.	3.
4.	4.

Being Aware

- Be careful of your thoughts (Head)
- Be aware of intuition (Heart)
- Lean into resistance (Blockage in Your Solar-Plexus or Stomach)

Expand Your Experience of Good

- Create a weekly gratitude list
- Say positive affirmations about yourself each day
- Have daily self-care routine

Vision Tracking

Positive Flow: What's coming in on my wish list? What do I need to lean into? What am I grateful for? How am I being supported?
- Week 1
- Week 2
- Week 3
- Week 4

Negative Flow: What's not working? Outside resistance? What do I need to let go of? Who do I need to stay away from that makes me feel unsupported?
- Week 1
- Week 2
- Week 3
- Week 4

This is where we learn to fly...
The Dove House
Healing & Wellness Beyond Recovery

Vital & Alive

(In 5 Minutes or Less)

Presented by
Kathleen Riley

Overview

✦ How Energy Centers Work
✦ Energy Flow
✦ Creating Safe Spaces
✦ Simple Energy Exercises for Wellbeing
✦ Gratitude, Blessings and Miracles

How Energy Centers Work?

- They are swirling disks with wide mouths that spin a few inches outside the body
- They draw energy stored from your emotional, mental, physical, and spiritual energy systems to nurture us wholly.
- There is a narrow funnel shaped tip that hooks directly into the spine
- They transmit information of past trauma and pain contained in imprint in the energy systems, into the nervous system

Source: Villoldo, Alberto, Ph.D., Shaman, Healer, Sage: How to Heal Yourself and Others

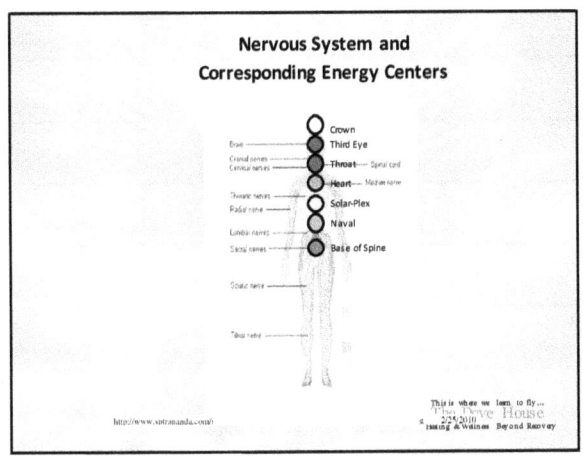

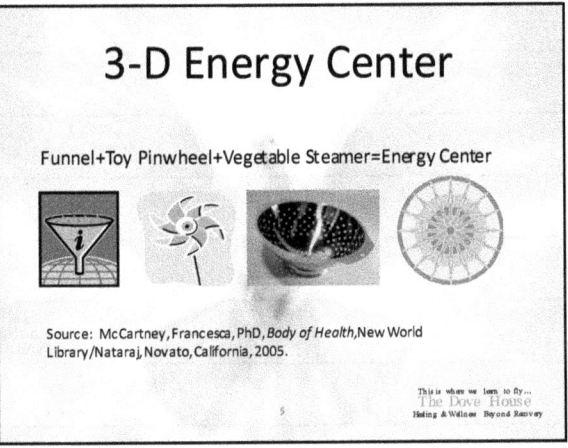

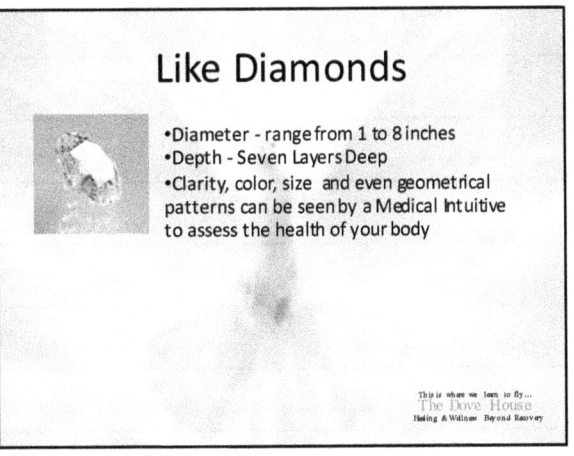

Seven Layers Deep

- 7th Layer holds the unfulfilled potential and stays dormant until the timing is right for it to blossom.
- Clearing and aligning the seven layers begins to correct alienation from your true self

Color & Clarity

- Color and clarity determines the health of your energy centers
- Color and clarity is generational, environmental, and relates to personal trauma.

Energy Flow

- Energy centers spin clockwise
- Energy travels up the left foot or base of the spin and winds around in a figure eight activating each energy center.
- Energy travels down the top of the head, winds around in a figure eight activating each energy center and moves down the right leg and out the foot.

Correcting Reverse Energy

- Rub or tap for 2 or 3 minutes the area underneath your collarbones; the center of your chest, above your heart; and underneath and two inches over from each breast.

Sweetening Spiral

- Offering acts of kindness, reaching out in love (sometimes as tough love), extending forgiveness, and moving into a place of acceptance.
- Positive actions beget positive reactions, which encourage us to again offer kindness, etc. etc.
- Able to maintain a synchronistic flow

Source: Benor Daniel J., MD, *Seven Minutes to Natural Pain Release*, Publications, Bellmawr, NJ, 2008.

Protection

- Visualize a violet energy coming in through your crown and allow the energy to flow down through the center of your body, passing from head to toe.
- Continue the flow down into the earth and securely fasten yourself.
- Expand the beam of light from your center into every cell of your body and into your auric field about four or eight feet in circumference.

Balance

- Inter-lock fingers together and thumbs side-by-side in an upright position.
- This position brings balance into your system in a matter of minutes.

Boundaries

- Gently tap on your 4th center for two to three minutes each day.
- Creates healthy boundaries and protects yourself from negative energies
- Balances your energy and helps you think more clearly

Grounding

- Visualizing an imaginary rope, vine or pole extending out the base of your spine and deep into the earth.
- Take your imaginary symbol as far down as you can go and fasten it to something secure like a rock or pole to tie it to.
- Feel the energy come up the base of your spine and allow it to expand like a balloon in your 1st energy center.
- Direct the energy up to your heart center and move it out your arms. Allow the rest of the energy to flow through your neck, head and out your crown.
- Visualize a fountain of gold pouring out and around your body as if there were a protective bubble surrounding you.

Source: McCartney, Francesca, PhD, *Body of Health*, New World Library/Nataraj, Novato, California, 2005.

Immune System Cleanse

- Direct the energy coming up your left leg, into your first center to cleanse your immune system, and then send the toxic energy out your right leg into the earth.
- Cleanses the first energy center where the immune system is located

Head & Heart Clearing

Good for Depression, Addiction, or Despair

- In a lying down position, place one hand on your heart and the other over your forehead.
- Use your fingers, as if they were a comb, and swipe the energy away from your body in a counter-clockwise motion at least four times.
- At the end of each set, take the dirty energy between your fingers and flick it away from your body.
- Repeat this exercise at least three times and remember to wash your hands when finished.
- It is also recommended you journal your thoughts, before or after, for additional clearing of mind and heart.

Gratitude, Blessings & Miracles

- Position one hand over heart center and the other hand palm down above the top of your head for 5 minutes or longer.
- Thank your Creator, God, or the Universe for all the beautiful wonders of your life.
- Bless your children, your relationship, and lessons learned.
- Thank God for peace, love, joy, and happiness each day regardless of any negative surroundings.

What to Remember...

- Energy awareness can bring balance, protection, grounding and healthy boundaries
- Acts of kindness, love, and forgiveness can create a sweetening spiral of positive reactions to life
- Energy exercises can boost the immune system
- Head & heart clearing can release depression, addiction, and despair
- Increase miracles by practicing gratitude and blessings daily

This is where we learn to fly...
The Dove House
Healing & Wellness Beyond Recovery

Presence for Protection

By Kathleen Riley

The Promise

Whoever dwells in the shelter of the Most High will rest in the shadow of the Almighty (Psalm 91:1)

How to Receive Presence

- Shift into a stream of wellbeing
- Believe in something greater than yourself
- Believe your prayers are already answered
- Ask for healing
- Create positive intentions

Victim-no-More

I celebrate life as a 'victim-no-more'.
I look for a direction that has flow, that has freedom.
I completely let go.
I give up all thinking with the rational mind, with no strategy and no motive directing me.
My prayers open me up, so my soul can see.
I run for the light.

-- Kathleen Riley
What You Feel is Real

Domestic Violence Story

Behavior Change
Reacting ➔ Acting

Flow of Well-Being

- Positive Friends & Family
- Support Groups
- Geographic Changes
- Spiritual Communities

Flow of Well-Being

"When, therefore, we were approached by those in whom the problem had been solved, there was nothing left for us but to pick up the simple kit of spiritual tools laid at our feet. We have found much of heaven and we have been rocketed into a fourth dimension of existence of which we had not even dreamed."

– The Big Book, Page 25

Home Invasion Story

Behavior Change
From Fearful ➔ To Empowerment

1 in 10 People Are Psychopaths

- Where the distinction between spirited and spiritless does come into play is in dealing with psychopathic people where even after promising to change they keep returning to their abusive ways
- When at some point, instead of realizing that they are just misguided and need even more time and attention, it is better to conclude that maybe they are acting perfectly in line with who they are.
- Naïve people who think everyone is equally good inside will keep rationalizing and taking the abuse, but those with higher understanding will recognize the warning signs of futility sooner and save themselves the trouble

Source: http://montalk.net/matrix/157/spiritless-humans

Spiritual Abnormalities

- Detached from self (more than one personality)
- Lacks empathy, remorse, or guilt
- Appears angry or cut-off from God
- Over Inflated or low self image
- Controlling and self-centered
- Extreme low-energy (They feel small, dirty, slithery)
- Extreme high-energy (Telepathic, trickery, magic, psychic abilities to control)
- What they say and do don't match up
- Critical of self and others
- Charming
- Lustful
- Lies
- Over generous with gifts
- Mocks your spirituality

Identifying Character Defects

- Jealousy
- Controlling behavior
- Quick involvement
- Unrealistic expectations
- Isolation of victim
- Blames others for his problems
- Blames others for his feelings
- Hypersensitivity
- Cruelty to animals or children
- Playful use of force during sex
- Verbal abuse
- Rigid sex roles
- Jekyll and Hyde type personality
- History of past battering
- Threats of violence
- Breaking or striking objects
- Forceful during an argument
- Objectification of women
- Tight control over finances
- Minimization of the violence
- Manipulation through guilt
- Extreme highs and lows
- Expects her to follow his orders
- Frightening rage
- Use of physical force
- Closed mindedness

Spiritual Abuse Story

Behavior Change
From Power Struggle →
To Stepping Out of the Cycle

Psychic Netting

- Creates spiritual radar between two people
- Made up of an invisible sticky substance similar to a spider's web
- Attaches itself to energy center receptors in the body's energy system
- Provides intelligence or intuitive hits about the other person in ways that are controlling

Detaching Visualization

1. Imagine clipping the invisible cords from the person who is attached to your energy receptors
2. Ask God to lift their net off your body
3. Imagine this substance returning to the person who originally sent it.
4. Bless them to become a positive force in the world.
5. Now imagine you are stepping into a body suit. Zip it up from your feet and to the top of your head.
6. Turn around and walk away in the opposite direction of the person.
7. Bless yourself and imagine only positive healthy relationships of love and connectedness in your life.

Breaking Invisible Ties

Negative Statement
"Even though I am bound by _____ twisted soul....I love myself wholly and completely and God loves me wholly and completely and unconditionally."

Positive Statement
I am free to love with sound mind, body and soul and believe God anoints me with a holy relationship and sacred union for the well-being of our selves, our families, and greater good in the world. ....I love myself wholly and completely and God loves me wholly and completely and unconditionally."

Affirmation Statement

"I am free from the invisible cords that bind me to _____ ; I am free to live fearlessly in a safe and peaceful existence… and I love myself wholly and completely and Christ loves me wholly and completely and unconditionally."

<u>Instructions</u>
Alternate tapping on right and left sides of legs until you believe the statement to be 100% true!

Practicing Presence

Increase Outer Presence

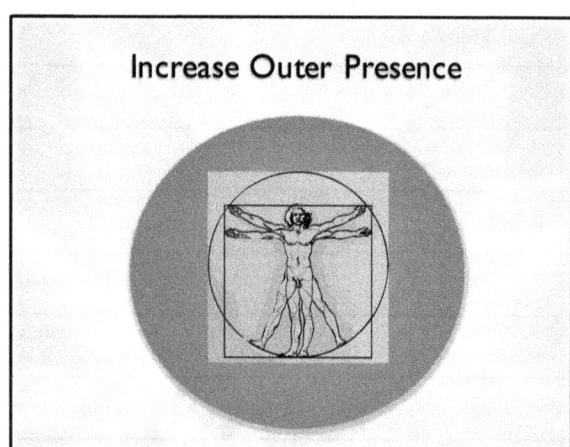

Enhance Your Environment

- Move away from depressed or low energy environments
- Create a sacred space in your home
- Use plants, flowers, essential oils to lift the environment
- Use color and special lighting to enhance the environment
- Organize, repair, or clean
- Move furniture around to create a sense of flow

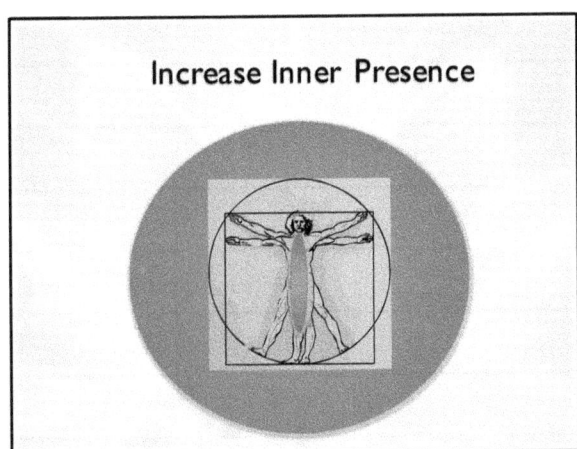

Increase Inner Presence

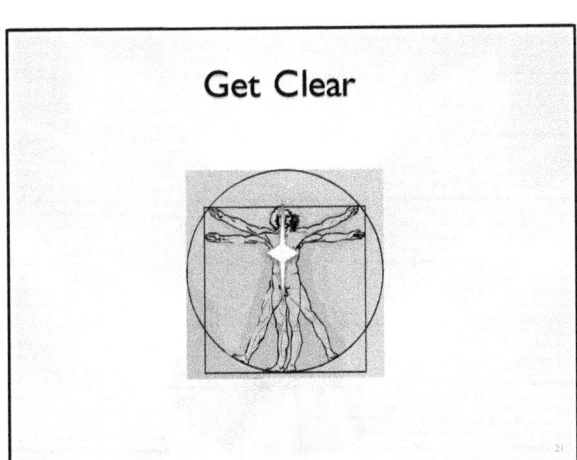

Get Clear

Strengthen

Child-Self
Abandoned
Dependent
Mentally Abused
Physically Abused
Controlled
Oppressed
Silenced

Adult-Self
Victim Mentality
Codependent
People Fixer
People Pleaser
Controlling
Depressed
Abusive

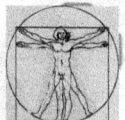
Greatest-Self
Open Hearted
Interdependent
Accepting
Compassionate
Personal
Responsibility
Joyful
Discerning
Creative

Lift Your Spirit

- Prayers, i.e. The Lord's Prayer (see prayer handout)
- Visualize a colorful bubble of protection around your body
- Visualize protecting yourself with a mantel or blanket
- Meditate consciously connecting with God and asking for His Protection
- Read inspirational materials/scripture
- Wear blessed medals
- Burn Incense

Heart Tapping for 3 Minutes

- Provides a protective shield
- Calms your mind
- Gives you the ability to think more clearly

Careful of Your Thoughts

- Thinking too much about the episode draws negativity into your life
- Romantic notions about the abuser brings that person back into your life
- Uncontrollable flashbacks recreates the story

Increasing Self Awareness

Level	Log	Emotion	Life View
Enlightenment	700 – 1000	Ineffable	Is
Peace	600	Bliss	Perfect
Joy	540	Serenity	Complete
Love	500	Reverence	Benign
Reason	400	Understanding	Meaningful
Acceptance	350	Forgiveness	Harmonious
Willingness	310	Optimism	Hopeful
Neutrality	250	Trust	Satisfactory
Courage	200	Affirmation	Feasible
Pride	175	Scorn	Demanding
Anger	150	Hate	Antagonistic
Desire	125	Craving	Disappointing
Fear	100	Anxiety	Frightening
Grief	75	Regret	Tragic
Apathy	50	Despair	Hopeless
Guilt	30	Blame	Evil
Shame	20	Humiliation	Miserable

Source: Hawkins, David, MD, *Power VS Force*

Disengage from Fear

Negative Statement
"Even though I fear I am at risk of losing my life, my house, my children, my job, and I feel desperate because ____, and I love myself wholly and completely and God loves me wholly and completely and unconditionally."

Positive Statement
I am free the fear of losing everything and feel a tremendous amount of support, love and safety in the world, and I love myself wholly and completely and God loves me wholly and completely and unconditionally."

Imagine a Sweetening Spiral

- Consciously reverse your direction and move up the spiral
- Create new realities and new improved life themes
- Get into the flow of well-being
- Create positive thoughts and feelings

St. Ignatius Prayer

"How can I respond to a God so good to me and surrounding me with the goodness of holy men and women and the wonderful gifts of creation?
All I can do is give thanks, wondering at God's forgiving love, which continues to give me life up to this moment."
St. Ignatius Loyola (Spiritual Exercises 61)

Sustain Goodness

- Presence
- Review
- Forgiveness
- Gratitude and Grace

Source: The Daily Examen, St. Ignatius Loyola

This is where we learn to fly...
The Dove House
Healing & Wellness Beyond Recovery

www.thedovehouse.org

Copyright © 2015, Kathleen Riley, LLC. All Rights Reserved

Trauma & Emotional Well-Being
In the New World of Healthcare

By Kathleen Riley

Copyright © 2015, Kathleen Riley, LLC. All Rights Reserved

Overview

- Effects of Trauma & Illness
- Energy Center Databases
- Emotional releasing methods for past trauma
- Relationship of emotional release to pain and Illness in the body

Effects of Trauma

- A University of Colorado study found that people who repressed their emotions after a traumatic event had lower immune systems than those who shared their feelings.
- The Journal of Psychosomatic Research reported that extreme suppression of anger was the most commonly identified characteristic of 160 breast cancer patients.

Roots of Illness

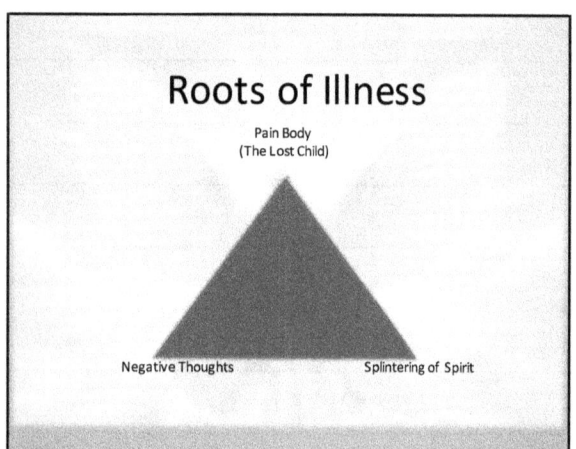

Pain Body (The Lost Child)

Negative Thoughts   Splintering of Spirit

Complex Energetic Database

- According to Dr. Caroline Myss, the human mind encodes thought, converts it into matter, and stores it within the body.
- These areas—also known as chakras—are the power centers of a complex energetic "database" that records your entire life.

Complex Energetic Database

After working with thousands of patients, Myss decoded the process of how these energy centers work – linked specific illnesses with past emotional traumas – and solved the puzzle of why some people heal, while others don't.

1st Energy Center

Energy Centers	Life Themes	Mental/Emotional Issues	Physical Dysfunctions
1	Safety in the physical world.	Physical family and group safety and security. Ability to provide for life's necessities. Ability to stand up for self. Feeling at home. Anxiety, stress, emotional and economic poverty beliefs. Social and familial law and order.	Chronic lower back pain. Sciatica, varicose veins. Rectal tumors, cancer, depression, and immune-related disorders.

2nd Energy Center

Energy Centers	Life Themes	Mental/Emotional Issues	Physical Dysfunctions
2	Power and control in the material world. Money sex and control of other people.	Blame and guilt. Sex, relationship and money. Ethics and honor in the relationship. Mood swings, depression. Overwhelming feelings of empathy. Inability to express emotions in a healthy way.	Chronic lower back pain, sciatica. Large and small intestines. Reproductive organs. Urinary system. Appendix and lower lumbar vertebra. OB/GYN issues and sexual dysfunction. Gastrointestinal issues include constipation, diarrhea, and gas. Chronic low back pain, sciatica, urinary problems. Lack of creativity. Inability to have positive sexual relationship.

3rd Energy Center

Energy Centers	Life Themes	Mental/Emotional Issues	Physical Dysfunctions
3	Personal power, fear of intimidation and rejection, Lack of self-esteem and survival intuitions.	Power struggles and associated anger. Low self-esteem, self-confidence and self-respect. Excessive generalized fear and difficulty making decisions. Oversensitive to criticism.	Gastric ulcers, pancreatitis and diabetes. Indigestion chronic or acute anorexia or bulimia, liver dysfunction, hepatitis, adrenal dysfunction, mid-back pain. Lethargy and morning fatigue.

4th Energy Center

Energy Centers	Life Themes	Mental/Emotional Issues	Physical Dysfunctions
4	All issues concerning love, compassion including creating from the heart, following your heart's desire, and love of other forms of life. Balance between caring for yourself and others.	Inability to feel or express love for self or others. Feelings of loss and grief. Anger, hatred, resentment, self-centeredness. Inability to forgive.	Congestive heart failure. Myocardial infarction (heart attack). Asthma, lung cancer and pneumonia. Upper back and shoulder problems. Breast cancer.

5th Energy Center

Energy Centers	Life Themes	Mental/Emotional Issues	Physical Dysfunctions
5	Development of will power. God's will. Creative expression and communication. Manifestation of the will in the physical form.	Fear of expression. Inability to speak your truth. Inability to bring your will forward in the world. Unwillingness to recognize and utilize your creativity.	Addiction and eating disorders.

6th Energy Center

Energy Centers	Life Themes	Mental/Emotional Issues	Physical Dysfunctions
6	The center of clairvoyance and intuition. Helps maintain a balance between intuition and analytical thought. Allows one to see the truth in situations. An openness to other people's ideas. Use of knowledge, higher reasoning and intuitive skills.	Dogmatic, judgmental thinking. Over-reliance on logic and analytical thought. Inability to see the truth in people or situations. Feelings of inadequacy. Inability to learn from experience.	Brain tumor, hemorrhage, stroke, and neurological disturbances. Blindness and deafness. Full spinal difficulties. Learning disabilities and seizures.

13

7th Energy Center

Energy Centers	Life Themes	Mental/Emotional Issues	Physical Dysfunctions
7	Acceptance of one's life. Capacity to fulfill one's purpose and find meaning in life. Knowingness and spiritual identity. Well-developed sense of self. Strong connection to your personal spirituality. Clear sense of your life path. Ability to see the larger picture. Importance of manifesting the spirit in physical reality.	Ability to trust life. Values, ethics, and courage. Humanitarianism. Selflessness, ability to see the larger patterns. Faith and inspiration. Spirituality and devotion. Lack of ability in trusting life. Diminished sense of self. Inability to take control of life. Unwillingness to recognize and connect with the spiritual element of life. Sense of not wanting to be a part of life, i.e. don't feel like you belong here.	Energetic Disorders. Mystical Depression. Chronic exhaustion that is not linked to a physical disorder. Extreme sensitivities to light, sound and other environmental factors.

14

Methods for Releasing Past Trauma

- Awareness of thoughts, feelings, and body pain
- Meditation, Journaling, Dream Work, Guided Imagery
- Holding or tapping energy centers corresponding to life themes and concerns
- Replacing negatives with positive affirmations and prayer

Vibrational Scale By Dr. David Hawkins

Vibrational Scale 1-1000	Vibration
Enlightenment	700-1000
Peace	600
Joy	540
Love	500
Reason	400
Acceptance	350
Willingness	310
Neutrality	250
Courage	200
Pride	175
Anger	150
Desire	125
Fear	100
Grief	75
Apathy	50
Guilt	30
Shame	20

Source: Power VS Force by David R Hawkins

Anger

Energy Center

Anger and resistance to caring for someone sick.   150

Pain

Anger and resistance to care for someone sick.   150

PAIN: Emotional Release comes with a jabbing pain in the 3rd & 4th Centers

Pain

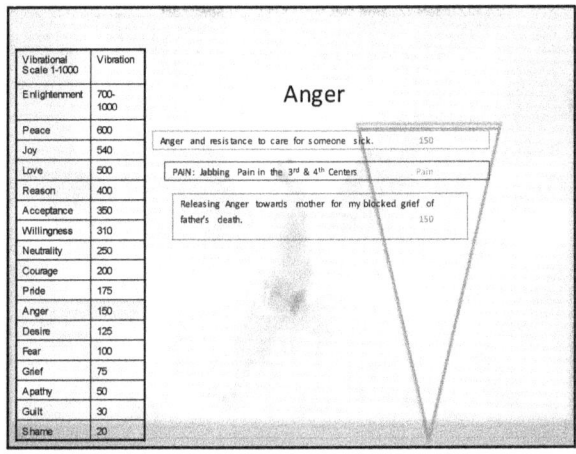

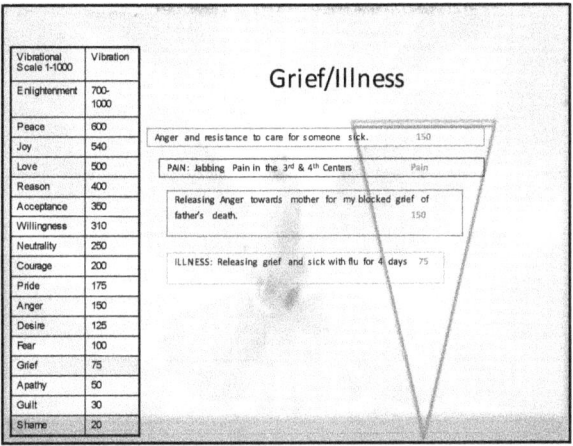

Abandonment

Vibrational Scale 1-1000	Vibration
Enlightenment	700-1000
Peace	600
Joy	540
Love	500
Reason	400
Acceptance	350
Willingness	310
Neutrality	250
Courage	200
Pride	175
Anger	150
Desire	125
Fear	100
Grief	75
Apathy	50
Guilt	30
Shame	20

Anger and resistance to care for someone sick.	150
PAIN: Jabbing Pain in the 3rd & 4th Centers	150
Anger comes up towards mother for blocking grieving of father's death.	150
ILLNESS: Releasing grief and becomes sick with flu for 4 days	75
PAIN: Resentment towards father because of alcoholism. Backache comes up between 2nd and 3rd Center	150
Abandonment comes up and released	100

Replaced with Acceptance

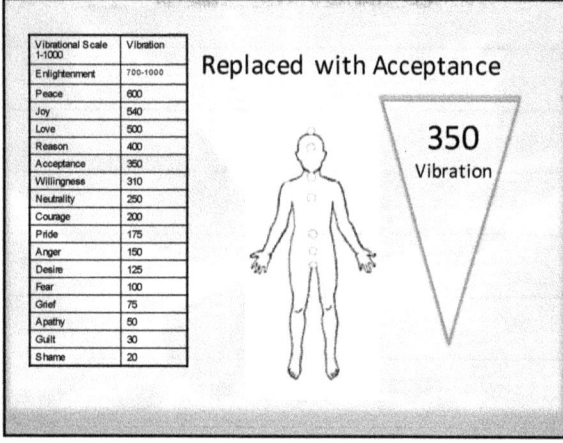

350 Vibration

What to Remember...

✧ The effects of trauma and illness on the body

✧ Energy centers are complex energetic databases

✧ Emotional releasing methods for past trauma

✧ Relationship of emotional release to pain and illness in the body

Pain: Your Opportunity to Heal

In the New World of Healthcare

By Kathleen Riley

Copyright © 2014, TLI, LLC. All Rights Reserved

Overview

- Pain Statistics & Pain Cycles
- Endorphins & Pain
- What is Pain Really About
- Talking to Your Pain
- How to Tap It Away!

Pain

- According to the National Center for Health Statistics (2006), approximately 76.2 million, one in every four Americans, have suffered from pain that lasts longer than 24 hours and millions more suffer from acute pain.
- Pain is cited as the most common reason Americans access the health care system.
- Pain affects more Americans than diabetes, heart disease and cancer combined.

Source: U.S. Department of Health & Human Services

Pain

- It is a leading cause of disability and it is a major contributor to health care costs.
- Chronic pain is the most common cause of long-term disability.

Source: U.S. Department of Health & Human Services

Prescription Painkillers

- 3 out of 4 prescription drug overdoses are caused by prescription painkiller
- 300% increase in overdose deaths since 1999
- 14,800 overdose deaths in 2008 (more than cocaine and heroin combined)

CDC Centers for Disease Control and Prevention

Prescription Painkillers

- 475,000 emergency department visits in 2009 (doubled in five years)
- 12M+ used prescription painkillers, none medically in 2010
- Half of prescription painkiller deaths involve at least one other drug

CDC Centers for Disease Control and Prevention

What is Pain?

"Pain is often a message from our inner self, spoken through the symptoms of our body."

--- Dr. Daniel Benor, M.D.

Vicious Circles of Pain

Tension muscles feel the pain:
- Emotional tension
- Anxiety
- More muscle tension
- Spasm

Source: Benor, Daniel J., MD, *Seven Minutes to Natural Pain Release*, Energy Psychology Press, 2008.

Roots of Illness

Pain Body
(Remembering the Lost Child)

Negative Thoughts   Splintering off of Spirit

Pain Is An Invitation To Heal

- Pain shows up in the present to get our attention from our past. We store emotions in our body from the past causing stress and tension in the present day, i.e. PTSD
- Pain shows up in the present to get our attention of what we fear in the future. Fear of the future freezes us in the present day with uncertainty, worry of the unknown, insecurity, self-doubt, or self-sabotaging behaviors, etc.

Sustained Positive Emotions

- Enhances synchronization of neurological activity and improves the cognitive function that generate rational thought, creativity and intentional action.
- Positive emotions give rise to a distinct mode of physiological functioning termed psychophysiological coherence.

Source: HeartMath Research Center, Institute of HeartMath, Boulder Creek CA.

Endorphins Naturally Manage Pain

- Endorphins are chemical messengers your body can create to help manage pain naturally.
- The more endorphins released into your system, the less pain you experience.

Source: Hearth Math.

Endorphins Naturally Manage Pain

- When endorphin levels fall, particularly during times of stress, aches and pains can increase.
- When these levels rise – exercising, listening to music or doing something as common and pleasurable as laughing – aches and pains diminish.
- Source: Hearth Math.

Pain Release Clues

- Physical Symptoms
- Imagery
- Dreams
- Archetype Patterns

Ask Your Physical Body…

- Put your hand on the area of pain, and ask your body, "What is it you would like me to know?" or "What are you trying to tell me?
- Be aware of a picture image or visional of words strung together in a sentence.
- The messages come from your intuitive brain not your thinking brain.

Talking to Your Pain

- Urinary Tract Infection: Ask yourself, "What are you upset about concerning relationship or sex?"
- Stomach Ache/Ulcers/Diarrhea: Ask yourself, "What are you worrying about concerning career, relationship, sex, or money.?"
- Skin Rash: Ask yourself, "Why are you disconnected from your greater self?
- Lower Back Pain: Ask yourself, "What is bothering you concerning family, money or a loved one?"

Talking to Your Back Pain

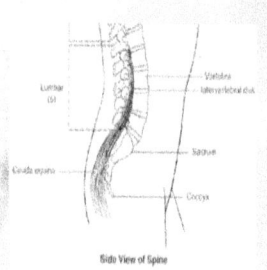

- L-1: Signifies a crying out for love. Needing to feel lonely. Lack of security.
- L-2: Signifies the inability to see a way out. Remaining stuck in pain from childhood.
- L-3: Signifies strong feelings of guilt and self-hatred. History of sexual abuse.
- L-4: Signifies one's rejection of her/his sexuality. Feeling financially insecure, and fearing having or changing careers. Strong feelings of powerlessness.

Talking to Your Back Pain

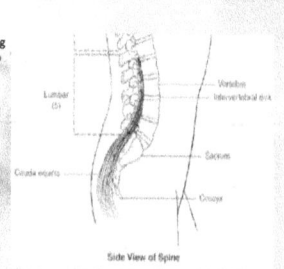

- L-5: Signifies feeling insecure. Difficulties in communicating. Strong feelings of anger. Denies the right to have pleasure in her/his life.
- Sacrum: Signifies stubbornly holding on to old anger. Feelings of powerlessness and loss of power.
- Coccyx (tailbone): Signifies blaming oneself, holding on to that which no longer serves theself, being out of balance with oneself, "sitting on old pain."

Source: Lower Back Pain Suggested by Louse Hay

Back Pain Release

Counteracting Statement
"Even though I feel pain in my lower back and I feel it represents my life load juggling everyday routines caring for two kids and trying to be all at all times... I love myself wholly and completely and God loves me wholly and completely and unconditionally."
4 Rounds: 10, 5, 3, 1

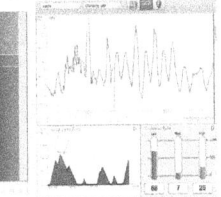

Back Pain Affirmation

Positive Statement
"I am pain free, I am flexible, and I am moving fearlessly... I love myself wholly and completely and God loves me wholly and completely and unconditionally."
3 Rounds: 7, 7, 7

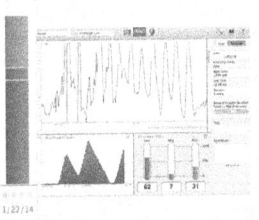

Positive Pain Release

- When pain comes up welcome it
- Resistance to pain will stop the correction the body is trying to achieve
- Meditate and allow the pain to move through your body
- Be aware of dream messages that guide the process
- Most unexplained pain is emotional

Gratitude Findings

- In an experimental comparison, those who kept gratitude journals on a weekly basis exercised more regularly, reported fewer physical symptoms, felt better about their lives as a whole, and were more optimistic about the upcoming week compared to those who recorded hassles or neutral life events (Emmons & McCullough, 2003).
- In a sample of adults with neuromuscular disease, a 21-day gratitude intervention resulted in greater amounts of high energy positive moods, a greater sense of feeling connected to others, more optimistic ratings of one's life, and better sleep duration and sleep quality, relative to a control group.
- Source: http://psychology.ucdavis.edu/Labs/emmons/PWT/index.cfm?Section=4
- UC Davis, Emmons Lab

Thank You for Protecting Me!

- Express gratitude for protection of self
- Express gratitude for protection from past generations
- Give permission for the protection to leave now

Connecting With Love

- See with your minds-eye who you want to embrace through love for a healing to take place.
- Create a positive intention for yourself and the people most closely associated with your pain.
- Hold the love in your heart with this intention while visualizing your loved ones who are involved for as long as you feel this healing is complete

Pain Release Protocol

1. Tap away pain as it relates to negative behaviors in your current state.
2. Tap away pain as it relates to negative behaviors in the current state that reminds you of past events.
3. Tap away negative behaviors that mirror what your parents and their parents passed on down to you.

Pain Release Protocol

4. Thank everyone for their part including loved ones who played a part in the story of your pain.
5. With gratitude tell them they can leave now. Say out loud, "It's okay, I don't need you anymore to protect me. You can leave my body."
6. Meditate on higher love visualizing yourself at the age when you first identified with the physical or emotional issue associated with the pain and other family members who contributed to the origin of the concern.

Be Mindful of Transference

- Pain
- Illness
- Emotions
- Thoughts

Questions to Ask

1. Get in touch with your body. If you are experiencing aches or pains, go there, and ask yourself, "Why?"
2. Ask yourself, "Is there something I can let go of from my past constricting the flow of my present?"
3. Be truthful with youself as difficult as it may seem. If it's heartache, address where it is in your heart? How deep is the pain? Is there something your heart would like to tell you?
4. Gauge your progress on whether the pain moves up, down, sideways or out. Movement is good.
Follow the direction of the pain and escort it out of your body.
5. Don't accept illness. You have the power to reverse the flow and dissolve "it".
6. Monitor your surroundings carefully. Stay away from critical people. Society embeds negative
emotions in your body via television, newspaper, internet, politics or work environment.
7. Use your whole body as a brain and your heart to filter thoughts.
8. Use your emotions to read a situation instead of being a victim of the situation.
9. Avoid pushing down feelings. They are only temporary and need to move through and out of the body.
10. Step into alignment with your life-purpose. Experience the wellness purpose can bring and be the miracle of 'you'.

What to Remember…

- Pain is a message from your body to release old tapes that no longer serve us.
- Pain is a message to release fears or protective modes that no longer serve us.
- Pain can be released with simple tapping methods of right and left brain stimulation.
- Pain goes away when practicing gratitude and appreciation
- Releasing old tapes opens the flow of health, vitality, and wellbeing with positive affirmations and love.

www.ingramcontent.com/pod-product-compliance
Lightning Source LLC
Chambersburg PA
CBHW080550170426
43195CB00016B/2739